MILWAUKEE

WHAT TO DO, WHERE TO GO, AND HOW TO HAVE FUN IN MILWAUKEE

by Sharon Hart Addy

John Muir Publications

Santa Fe, New Mexico

John Muir Publications,
P.O. Box 613, Santa Fe, NM 87504

Printed in the United States of America
First edition. First printing August 1997

ISBN 1-56261-362-6

Editors Dianna Delling, Marybeth Griffin
Graphics Editor Tom Gaukel, Joanne Thomas
Production Marie J.T. Vigil, Nikki Rooker
Cover Design Caroline Van Remortel
Typesetting Diane Rigoli
Illustrations Stacy Venturi-Pickett
Maps Susan Harrison
Printer Hi-Liter Graphics/Burton & Mayer
Front Cover Photo © Todd Dacquisto/Third Coast Stock
    Source
Back Cover Photo © Dr. J.W. Franta/Schlita Audubon
    Center

Kidding Around is a registered trademark of
John Muir Publications.

Distributed to the book trade by
Publishers Group West
Emeryville, California

*While every effort has been made to provide accurate,
up-to-date information, the author and publisher accept
no responsibility for loss, injury, or inconvenience
sustained by any person using this book.*

About the Author:
Sharon Hart Addy, a resident of the Milwaukee area, is a
freelance writer and mother of two. Her work has appeared
in *Highlights for Children* and other magazines for adults and
children. Sharon's previously published children's books
include *A Visit with Great-Grandma* and *We Didn't Mean To.*

C O N T E N T S

1/ Welcome to Milwaukee! 1

2/ Parks and the Great Outdoors 12

3/ Animals, Animals 28

4/ Landmarks, Skyscrapers, and the Arts 42

5/ Good Sports 58

6/ Museums and More 72

7/ That's Entertainment 88

8/ Let's Eat! 104

Calendar of Milwaukee Events 114

Resource Guide: When, What, and Where? 117

Answers to Puzzles 126

Geographical Index 132

Index 133

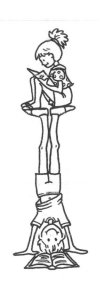

COLOR THE ROUTE
FROM YOUR HOMETOWN TO MILWAUKEE

If you're flying, color the states you'll fly over.
If you're driving, color the states you'll drive through.
If you live in Wisconsin, color the states you have visited.

WELCOME TO MILWAUKEE!

YOU'RE STANDING BAREFOOT ON THE wet, packed sand of McKinley Beach. Waves swirl around your toes. Out on the lake, sailboats race with the wind. You turn and run back to your towel. Beyond the beach, the street is full of cars, vans, and bicycles. Across the street, on the bluff, buildings reach to the sky. Milwaukee is a combination of quiet places and busy ones.

⬆ **A glimpse of Milwaukee's skyline and Lake Michigan**

Milwaukee is the largest city in Wisconsin. To find Milwaukee on a map, look along the border of the United States and Canada. You'll find the Great Lakes. Next, find the lake that points north and south. If you found Lake Michigan, you found the right lake. Milwaukee is on the west side of the lake in the southeast corner of Wisconsin.

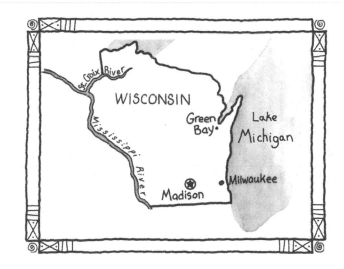

MILWAUKEE, THE CITY OF FESTIVALS!

In summer, festivals take place all over Milwaukee. Some have carnival rides; others have playgrounds. Many offer special activities for kids.

Milwaukee is known for its German heritage, but people from all over the world live here. They remember their homelands with celebrations. Festivals like **German Fest** and **Indian Summer** give you a chance to try ethnic foods, watch folk dances, look at displays, and do some shopping.

Not all festivals are ethnic, of course. **Summerfest** is a summer event celebrating all kinds of music. During **Winterfest**, you can ice-skate at Cathedral Square.

In July the circus spends a week in Milwaukee. At the circus grounds you can see the animals and circus wagons, and watch the show under the Big Top. Circus week ends with the **Great Circus Parade** down Wisconsin Avenue.

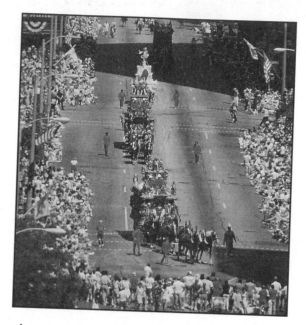

↑ **The Great Circus Parade**

The wagons and animals for the Circus Parade come to Milwaukee by train from the Circus World Museum in Baraboo.

INDIANS, FUR TRADERS, AND THE GREAT BRIDGE WAR

Menominee and Potawatomi Indians once lived where Milwaukee is today. Hunting and fishing were good then. Wild rice grew in swamps along the river.

In the early 1800s, two towns were settled along the Milwaukee River. Fur trader Solomon Juneau started Juneautown on the river's east side, and Byron Kilbourn set up Kilbourntown on the west side. People used boats to travel between the towns.

When someone suggested building a bridge, both Juneau and Kilbourn refused. They wanted their towns to remain separate. Kilbourn even designed his roads so they wouldn't end across from Juneau's.

⬆ **Children prepare for Indian Summer, an annual celebration of Native American culture.**

The earliest Indians in this part of Wisconsin built mounds in the shapes of animals and birds.

Bridges were built and wrecked. One night the people of Juneautown even pointed a cannon at Kilbourntown. The cannon was never fired.

Finally, the two settlements became Milwaukee. Bridges were built connecting the roads on either side of the river. You'll notice that Milwaukee's downtown bridges still cross the river at an angle.

A City of Immigrants

Farmers from the east coast of the United States were among the first settlers in Milwaukee. These "Yankees" wanted to farm fields without so many rocks.

Across the Atlantic Ocean, the Irish were starving. They heard about Milwaukee and came. People from other countries came, too.

The Germans that came to Milwaukee put up buildings like the ones they had in

⇑ **St. Josaphat's Basilica is a cultural monument as well as a place of worship.**

About 617,000 people live in the city of Milwaukee today.

Germany. They prepared their favorite foods, including bratwurst, and brewed beer. Polish immigrants settled on the south side of Milwaukee. They built **St. Josaphat's Basilica** so they would have a beautiful church.

Other groups—Italians, Mexicans, Puerto Ricans, Palestinians, and Asians— came and stayed, too.

People from other parts of the United States and around the world still come to Milwaukee. As the city changes, each nationality adds to the mixture of people and ideas that make up the city.

COLOR THE FLAG

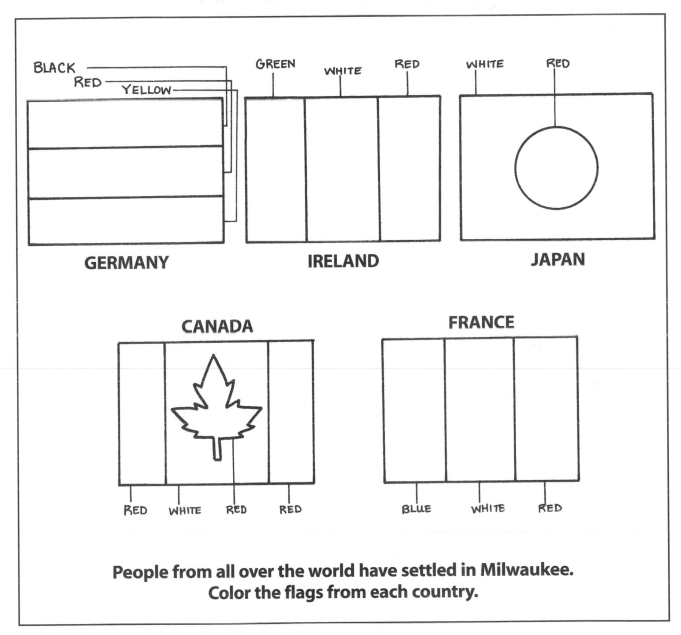

BLACK
RED
YELLOW

GERMANY

GREEN   WHITE   RED

IRELAND

WHITE   RED

JAPAN

CANADA

RED   WHITE   RED   RED

FRANCE

BLUE   WHITE   RED

**People from all over the world have settled in Milwaukee.
Color the flags from each country.**

THE PORT OF MILWAUKEE AND THE ST. LAWRENCE SEAWAY

In the early days of Milwaukee, only ships from ports on the Great Lakes sailed to Milwaukee. In 1959 the St. Lawrence Seaway opened, allowing ships from the Atlantic Ocean to reach the Great Lakes.

Today ships from France, Belgium, Great Britain, Turkey, Canada, and Brazil stop here. They deliver manufactured goods, steel, sand, salt, coal, and other products. When they leave they take manufactured goods and grain back to their own countries.

⇡ **The Hoan Bridge arches over the entrance to the Port of Milwaukee.**

The **Port of Milwaukee** is also a railroad transfer center. Containers taller than a basketball player and as long as a house (8 feet wide, 8 feet tall, and 20 or 40 feet long) come by rail from Canada and are switched to other trains, ships, or trucks. It's fun to guess what's in the containers. Good guesses include clothing, electronics, leather, and wood products.

⇡ **What could this ship be loading at the dock?**

The ocean-going ships you might see in Milwaukee can be up to 730 feet long. That's about 2 football fields.

CROSSWORD FUN

Shipping is an important activity in Milwaukee. Solve this crossword by figuring out the clues or completing the sentences. If you need help, use the clue box.

Clue Box

coal	Michigan
fish	port
grain	steel
Great	train
Lawrence	

Across

3. This vehicle travels on railroad tracks.

6. The St. _____ Seaway allows ships to sail from Milwaukee to the Atlantic Ocean.

7. Ships share the waters with these scaly, swimming creatures that breath through gills.

8. A _____ is a town or city where ships unload and take on cargo.

9. Rye, oats, corn, wheat, and other types of _____ are grown on Wisconsin farms then loaded onto ships in Milwaukee.

Down

1. This black substance is burned for fuel. Naughty children might also find it in their stockings on Christmas morning.

2. Ships bring this strong metal product to Milwaukee, where it is used to build sky scrapers and office buildings.

4. Milwaukee is located on Lake _____.

5. Lakes Huron, Ontario, Michigan, Erie, and Superior are known as the _____ Lakes.

MILWAUKEE INDUSTRY

Milwaukee is known for brewing beer, but other things are also made here. Have you heard of **Harley-Davidson** motorcycles? They're from Milwaukee. So are **Master Lock** bike chains and combination locks, and **Koss** headphones. **Red Star Yeast**, which is widely used for baking bread, is from this city, too.

Ambrosia Chocolate is a company that imports cocoa beans and makes chocolate for the baking industry. The flavoring in your chocolate cupcake might come from Milwaukee!

Milwaukee factories make car batteries, car frames, electrical tools, lawn mower engines, delicate instruments that control temperature, airplane parts, and machines for industry. Knit clothing like scarves, mittens, and caps are also made here.

⬆ **Milwaukee is the home of the Harley-Davidson Company.**

With the help of a mechanic, Christopher Latham Sholes invented the typewriter in Milwaukee in 1867.

Central Milwaukee

MILWAUKEE'S WEATHER

Milwaukee has all four seasons. Trees bud in spring, fill with leaves in summer, drop their leaves in fall, and are bare in winter. Each season has a good mix of sunshine and rain or snow.

Summer days are usually warm, with temperatures ranging from the 70s to sometimes over 100. But when the sun goes down in June and July, it gets chilly. August can be hot and humid, day and night.

If you're going out on Lake Michigan in a boat, take a sweatshirt. Even on hot days, it can be cold on the lake. Spring and fall are jacket weather, and if you visit during the winter, bring warm clothes. Winter temperatures go from the 30s to below freezing. When it's really cold, you need to bundle up!

Summertime weather forecasts often end with the words "cooler by the lake."

A snowy day in Lake Park

That's because a cool wind often blows off Lake Michigan. If you're at the beach you'll be cool, even if it's hot in the rest of the city. In the winter, the lake breeze brings snow to places along the shore. This snow that blows in off the lake is called "lake effect" snow.

Downtown Milwaukee

2 PARKS AND THE GREAT OUTDOORS

WHAT ARE YOU LOOKING FOR? SANDY BEACHES and fishing? Baseball diamonds and basketball courts? Or would you prefer nature walks, bike trails, and outdoor concerts?

The Milwaukee County Park System offers all of these and more. Parks line the lakefront, and there are plenty inland, too. The Oak Leaf Trail, which connects the parks, has more than 96 miles of paths for bicyclists, joggers, and in-line skaters.

In winter some of the park lagoons become ice-skating rinks. Hills and trails are groomed for sledding and cross-country skiing.

Many of the parks offer children's programs, free concerts, and movies. Call (414) 257-4503 to hear a recording of special events.

↑ **Flower gardens inside one of the Mitchell Park Domes**

Parks and the Great Outdoors

1. **Bradford Beach**
2. **Lake Park**
3. **McKinley Beach**
4. **McKinley Marina**
5. **Mitchell Park and Domes**
6. **Riverwalk & Pere Marquette Park**
7. **Veteran's Park**
8. **Whitnall Park, Boerner Botanical Gardens, Wehr Nature Center**

Lake Michigan

General Mitchell International Airport

N

43
41
794
94
894

St
St
N 27th St
N M.L. King Jr.
N Humbolt Blvd
N Prospect Av
N Lake Dr
Lincoln Memorial Dr
Water St
Hoan Bridge
S 1st St
S 16th St
S 60th St
S 108th
S 92nd
Clement Av
Superior St
S Pennsylvania Av
S Lake Dr
Whitnall Av
Airport St
N 27th St
National
Mitchell St
Home Av
Howard Av
Forest St
Grange Av
Rawson Av

VETERAN'S PARK

The breeze on the lakefront makes it a perfect place to fly a kite. Veteran's Park even has a special kite-flying area. If you forgot your kite, you can buy one there at a store called **Gift of Wings**.

Joggers, walkers, cyclists, and skaters use the paved **Oak Leaf Trail** that crosses Veteran's Park. At **High Rollers** you can rent bikes, roller blades, or roller skates and join them!

For water fun, rent a paddle boat and go out on the lagoon. If you just want to relax, you can sit back and watch sailboats racing the wind on the lake. The **Milwaukee Community Sailing Center** offers lessons and rentals to teens and adults. It also holds week-long sailing lessons for children at inland lagoons.

⬆ **The Oak Leaf Trail is a great place to ride a bike.**

The monument in Veteran's Park honors men and women who died in the Vietnam War.

MATCH THE KITES

Find the kite on the left that matches the one on the right. Then connect the matching kites with a line. Color in the scene when you're finished.

McKINLEY MARINA AND BEACH

Boats, boats, and more boats! McKinley Marina has all kinds of privately owned boats. Grab a snack at the concession area and watch them come and go. Some are charter boats that take people fishing out on Lake Michigan.

McKinley Beach is just north of McKinley Marina. Breakwaters on each end of the beach protect the shore from the biggest waves. The sand here is just right for building castles, so bring a pail and shovel, or a few soda cups. Just don't forget to take your sand tools with you when you leave the beach.

The observation area on the north side of the beach lets you look down into the restless waves. The stony beach on the other side of the observation area is used by windsurfers. They're fun to watch, too.

Lake Michigan is the third largest of the Great Lakes. It's one of the biggest freshwater lakes in the world.

⇑ **A busy boating day on Lake Michigan**

WHAT'S THE DIFFERENCE?

**These two pictures of the beach might look the same, but they're not.
How many differences between the two scenes can you find?
Hint: There are at least 10 differences.**

BRADFORD BEACH

↥ **Members of the Polar Bear Club take an icy dunk.**

Bradford Beach is the most popular beach in the city. On a hot day, people lie in the sun and let the lake breeze cool them off. Even on hot days in early summer you won't see many people in the water. Lake Michigan is so cold that the water doesn't warm up until late July. The **Polar Bear Club** goes for a swim each year on New Year's Day. Brrrr!

The Bradford Beach bathhouse was built in the 1940s. It is supposed to be shaped like a riverboat, but you'll have to use your imagination to see it as a boat.

If you get hungry you can run over to the North Point concession stand next to the beach. They have hot dogs, hamburgers, and other snack foods.

The Pro Beach Volleyball Tournament is held on Bradford Beach in mid-June.

WHERE'S MY TOWEL?

This polar bear is trying to find his way to his towel after a chilly swim. Can you help him?

LAKE PARK

Lake Park is on the bluff overlooking the lake. The best way to explore this park is by foot. Notice the landscape as you walk down the paths through the woods. This is what the Milwaukee area looked like to early settlers.

The path running along the golf course leads to the **North Point Lighthouse**. Walk past the stone lions and cross the bridge over the ravine. The lighthouse was built over 100 years ago. It once used an oil burning lantern, but now it's electric. On clear nights, the light can be seen 25 miles out on the lake.

Stop to watch the lawn bowlers across from the golf course. Lawn bowling is an outdoor game that doesn't involve bowling pins. Instead, players take turns throwing colored balls on the grass.

You'll find playground equipment on the north end of the park, in Area 3.

North Point Lighthouse helps nighttime boaters find their way.

HIDE AND SEEK

There are 13 objects hidden in this forest scene. After you've circled the hidden objects, color the scene. Look for: cup, spoon, scissors, airplane, tennis shoe, pencil, mouse, coffee pot, donkey head, baseball bat, fork, cap, and button.

Each dome in Mitchell Park is as tall as a 7-story building.

Together, the domes feature more than 4,000 different kinds of plants.

MITCHELL PARK AND "THE DOMES"

When you see the three domes you'll know you're near Mitchell Park and the **Mitchell Park Horticultural Conservatory**. Horticulture is the science and art of growing fruits, vegetables, and flowers or ornamental plants.

The tropical dome is like a mini rain forest. You'll see a waterfall and banana trees, along with birds, lizards, and frogs.

The desert dome is hot and dry, the perfect place for palm trees and cactus. Did you know cactus could be so big, and so small?

The flowers and scenery in the third dome change five times a year. Who knows what you'll see during your visit!

Outside the domes, there's a lagoon for fishing, a playground, a wading pool, tennis courts, a ball diamond, and picnic tables. During the winter, the lagoon freezes and becomes an ice-skating rink.

LOOKING IN THE GARDEN

Hidden in this word search are 10 garden words. Search for words vertically, horizontally, and diagonally. Can you find all of them? The first word has been found for you.

Word Box

banana	flower	violets
bloom	grow	water
cactus	palm tree	
desert	rain forest	

```
A P S S A R A I N F O R E S T
B A I W O Q W S E A D B A N T
A L V L K F W J S S E V D N V
X M P A M C A C T U S X S O I
B T L C D A J L E O E O R O O
V R E E A R L S G A R E F K L
B E S L J A S Z U Y T B L I E
N E Y C N H T E I A J L Z K T
J D A A H E I R W I K O T E S
V H N K E Y T F O F L O W E R
G A L A O V E O B E L M E W W
B O S H T S G R O W Z O S T W
```

THE RIVERWALK AND PERE MARQUETTE PARK

Just because you're in the middle of the city, you don't have to stay indoors.

The **Riverwalk** follows the Milwaukee River through the heart of downtown. While you walk, you can watch the river, the boats, the gulls, and the ducks. Several boat tours leave from docks along the river.

When you're ready to eat, you can pick up lunch from one of the shops on Old World Third Street or the Grand Avenue Mall. You can also stop at one of the restaurants along the way.

The pavilion at **Pere Marquette Park** on the Riverwalk marks the spot where Father Jacques Marquette, a French explorer and missionary, pulled his birch-bark canoe on shore in 1674 and set up camp. Wouldn't he be surprised if he arrived today during a free concert or movie?

⇑ **Joggers are a common sight around the Riverwalk.**

Milwaukee's Marquette University is named in honor of Father Marquette.

← **Live entertainment at Pere Marquette Park's pavilion**

CAN YOU CANOE?

Many early explorers used this type of boat to navigate rivers and creeks. Color the shapes with numbers brown. Color the shapes with letters blue. If a shape doesn't have a letter or number, use any color you want.

WHITNALL PARK

Whitnall Park was named after Charles A. Whitnall. He thought up the idea of putting Milwaukee's parks along rivers and creeks.

Boerner (BURN-er) **Botanical Gardens** is on the top of the hill in the park. Some people come here just to smell the roses, but there are lots of other flowers, too. The rock garden has a waterfall and wildflowers. The stone steps from the rock garden lead to the bog walk. A bog is a wet, spongy area of land with lots of plants. Don't worry about getting your shoes wet—there are bridges to keep your toes dry.

Save some energy for a visit to the **Wehr** (pronounced WHERE) **Nature Center.** Trails here wander through areas representing prairielands, wetlands, and woodlands. Programs for kids and grown-ups are held all year-round.

⬆ **Whitnall Park is prettiest when its flowers are in bloom.**

Glaciers scraped across Wisconsin during the Ice Age. When they melted, they left piles of gravel we see as hills.

MY TRAVEL JOURNAL
—Parks and the Great Outdoors—

I had fun when I visited: _____

I learned about: _____

My favorite park was: _____

This is a picture of what I saw at a park in Milwaukee •••

3 ANIMALS, ANIMALS

WHENEVER YOU'RE OUTSIDE IN MILWAUKEE, watch for animals. What you see will depend on where you are, the time of day, and the season.

Most places in the area have crows, geese, pigeons, robins, starlings, squirrels, and gulls. In parks look for garden snakes, rabbits, blue jays, and mourning doves. In grassy fields you might see butterflies, hawks, grasshoppers, deer, woodchucks, spiders, red foxes, coyotes, and meadowlarks.

In the woods be alert for owls, woodpeckers, chipmunks, raccoons, toads, salamanders, chickadees, millipedes, and bats. In wet places check for dragonflies, frogs, turtles, kingfishers, mosquitoes, mallards, muskrats, and red-winged blackbirds.

Along Lake Michigan look for ducks, copepods, mayflies, and clams. If you could see into the lake, you would find salmon, trout, and perch.

⇡ **Deer and other wildlife can been seen at the Schlitz Audubon Center.**

Animals, Animals

1. Green Meadows Farm
2. Havenwoods State Forest
3. Milwaukee County Zoo
4. Schlitz Audubon Center
5. Scout Lake
6. Timber Wolf Preservation Society

THE MILWAUKEE COUNTY ZOO

What's the difference between a monkey and an ape? You'll learn when you visit the Primate House at the zoo.

To peek inside a lake, stop at the Lake Wisconsin Aquarium. The anaconda, Chinese alligator, and other reptiles live in this building, too. In the small mammal building you can see bats and other night animals while they're active.

Some animals who are neighbors in the wild live together in big, open spaces at the zoo. Ostriches, antelope, zebra, and stork gather at an African water hole. Their enemy, the African lion, roams nearby.

The children's area has a working dairy farm, and special warm-weather shows feature sea lions and birds of prey.

This pair of seals is sitting pretty at the Milwaukee Zoo.

The Milwaukee County Zoo is one of many organizations helping to save the Humboldt penguin from extinction.

COLOR TO FIND THE ANSWER

Which animal is often called "The King of the Beasts"? To find the answer, color all the shapes with the letter A orange. Color all the shapes with the letter B brown. Color all the shapes with the letter C black.

SCHLITZ AUDUBON CENTER

The Schlitz Audubon Center is a great place to visit even when the weather isn't nice. From inside the building, you'll see chipmunks, squirrels, birds, and sometimes deer or raccoons at the bird feeder. Check out the "Please Touch" table, the wall displays, and the puzzles and quizzes. Pick up a copy of *Center Focus* to see what programs are coming up.

If you're ready to walk, take the beach path. Watch for gulls, ducks, and driftwood, and check the sand for animal tracks. Climb to the top of the lookout tower and you can see for miles around. Follow the paths through the grasslands, prairie, or ravine loops. Walk quietly, and stop to look and listen.

⬆ **Admiring a toad at the Schlitz Audubon Center**

Schlitz Audubon Center's "Nature Now" phone number is (414) 352-8833. The recorded message gives facts about nature in the area.

UNSCRAMBLE THE WORDS

CACONRO _____

XFO _____

PICUKHMN _____

EDRE _____

RBID _____

The animal names on the left are all mixed up. Unscramble the names, then draw a line from the name to the correct picture on the right.

HAVENWOODS STATE FOREST

The land at Havenwoods State Forest once held prison buildings, a missile site, and even a city landfill. After these things were removed, the land was left vacant. Now the woods and fields are home to deer, red foxes, opossums, raccoons, mice, voles, bats, great horned owls, and red-tailed hawks.

This is a big area. If you bring a bicycle, you can ride the limestone paths. But before you hit the trails, stop at the center's information desk and ask for a guide. It tells about plants that are not native to our country, and shows bird and animal tracks to watch for.

"Like winds and sunsets, wild things were taken for granted until progress began to do away with them."
—Aldo Leopold,
A Sand Country Almanac

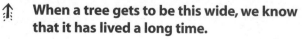

When a tree gets to be this wide, we know that it has lived a long time.

CROSSWORD FUN

Havenwoods State Forest is the perfect place for nature lovers. Solve this crossword by figuring out the clues or completing the sentences. If you need help, use the clue box.

Down

1. Birds build _____ in the branches of tall trees.
3. Bambi is the most famous of these animals.
5. This fungus, also known as a toadstool, grows in dark, damp parts of the forest.

Across

2. A green _____ may turn red, orange, or brown when autumn comes.
4. Oak, elm, and maple are types of _____.
5. These tiny rodents scurry across the forest floor.
6. An animal's footprints, or _____, are easy to see after the snow falls.
7. The great _____ owl seems to ask, "who?"
8. Squirrels nibble these nuts that fall from oak trees.

Clue Box

acorns	leaf	nests
deer	mice	tracks
horned	mushroom	trees

SCOUT LAKE

Even though Scout Lake is in a busy part of the city, it is not easy to find. It's a quiet spot to have a picnic, take a walk, play on the playground, or go fishing. The lake has rainbow trout, bass, walleye, sauger, bluegill, crappie, bullheads, sunfish, and yellow perch. Bring a pole and pick a spot on the pier. Kids under 16 don't need a license to fish here.

If the fish aren't biting, take a hike. A paved walkway circles the lake. Other paths lead off into the trees. If you follow them you'll be treated to the "caw, caw, caw" of a crow or the "rat-ta-tat-tat" of a woodpecker. Watch the ground for squirrels, chipmunks, and other little creatures.

⇧ **Learn to cast your line at a Scout Lake fishing clinic.**

Drifting in a paddleboat on Scout Lake lets you watch for fish.

CATCH OF THE DAY

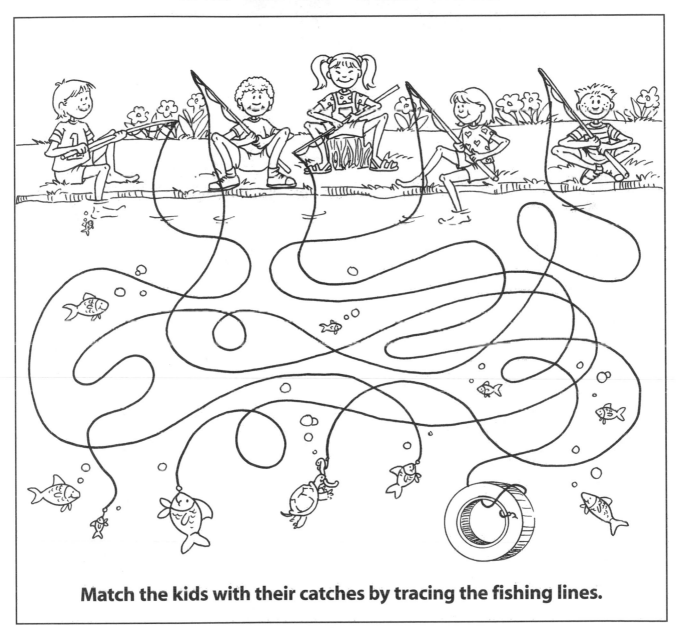

Match the kids with their catches by tracing the fishing lines.

GREEN MEADOWS FARM

Have you ever hugged a goat? Caught a chicken? Milked a cow? The people at Green Meadows Farm will help you do those things.

Over 300 animals, including sheep, turkeys, geese, and donkeys, live on this farm. There are more unusual animals, too, like the ostrich and the pot-bellied pigs. A guide will take you around, answer your questions, and tell you about the animals.

A hayride is included in the tour. Big tractors pull wagon-loads of kids and adults. There are pony rides, too (for kids only). When the ride is over you can go back to look at the animals.

Baby animals have special name. Baby horses are called *foals*. Baby pigs are *piglets,* and baby goats are *kids*.

GREEN MEADOWS FARM

ROESH _____

OGAT _____

WOC _____

DKCU _____

HCNECIK _____

IGP _____

chick

foal

calf

piglet

duckling

kid

Sometimes baby animals have special names. First, unscramble the animal names. Then draw a line to match the animal name to the name of it's offspring

THE TIMBER WOLF PRESERVATION SOCIETY

Long ago, wolves lived all over North America. Their silent step, strong sense of smell, and swiftness made them good hunters. As farms and towns spread across the country, people thought wolves were a danger to them. Today the wolf is an endangered species.

Jim Rieder wanted to learn more about wolves. He dreamed of raising wolves and setting them free in the wild. His dream led to the Timber Wolf Preservation Society. Even though the Society's wolves are fed and cared for by people, they are wild animals. The wolves look like big shaggy dogs, but they're shy, and some of the cubs only peek out at visitors. Yearlings and adult wolves often move gracefully around their enclosures. If you're quiet, they may stop to stare at you.

Timber wolves live seven to ten years in the wild. They can live up to 16 years in captivity.

⬆ Thor, Niko, Dakota, and Denali are wolves at the Timber Wolf Preservation Society.

MY TRAVEL JOURNAL

—Animals, Animals—

I had fun when I visited: _____

I learned about: _____

_____

My favorite animal was: _____

This is a picture of an animal I saw

LANDMARKS, SKYSCRAPERS, AND THE ARTS

THE MILWAUKEE SKYLINE IS A MIXTURE OF OLD AND new buildings. You'll see flat roofs, rounded domes, and pointed spires. Notice the revolving restaurant on the Hyatt-Regency Hotel. It looks a bit like a flying saucer.

The tallest building in Milwaukee, the Firstar Center, has 42 floors. Another building, the Wisconsin Gas Building, has a flame-shaped light on top. When it is lit, it tells the weather. Red means it will get warmer, gold signals colder, and blue says the temperature will stay the same.

City Hall is the seventh tallest building in Milwaukee. When it was built, in 1895, it was the third tallest building in the United States.

While you're looking up, look for stone carvings. The carved figures with the funny-looking faces are called gargoyles.

⇧ **The Wisconsin Gas Building shines brightly at night.**

Milwaukee has many statues and sculptures. The orange sculpture at the end of Wisconsin Avenue sparked a lot of argument when it was first erected.

Hwy 145

Fond du Lac Freeway

Hampton Av

W Fond du Lac Av

Capitol Dr

Lisbon Av

92nd St

St

43

Kilbourn Av

N Old World Third St

E Wells

Cathedral Square

N Jackson St

St

N Van Buren

N Prospect Av

Veteran's Park

The Grand Avenue

N Plankinton Av

N Water St

E Wisconsin Av

E Michigan St

Cass St

N Harbor Dr

Lake Michigan

Milwaukee River

N Lake Dr

N Prospect Av

N Lincoln Memorial Dr

N 12th St

Av

Av

Av

N Water St

N Hoan Bridge

Lake Michigan

Mitchell

S 1st St

27th St

16th St

794

Landmarks, Skyscrapers, and the Arts

1. Allen Bradley Clock Tower
2. Firstar Center
3. General Mitchell International Airport
4. Hoan Bridge
5. Hyatt Regency Hotel
6. Milwaukee City Hall
7. North Point Water Tower
8. Pabst Mansion
9. St. Joan of Arc Chapel
10. War Memorial Center and Milwaukee Art Museum
11. Wisconsin Gas Building

N

ALLEN BRADLEY CLOCK TOWER

If you are on the south side of Milwaukee and need to know the time, look for The Allen Bradley Clock Tower. On clear nights, the clock tower can be seen from 30 miles out on the lake. Boaters look for the tower to figure out where they are. The clock is the largest four-faced clock in the world. Just how big is it?

★ The triangles marking the hours are 4 feet long.

★ Each hour hand is 15 feet, 9 inches long and weighs 490 pounds.

★ Each minute hand is 20 feet long and weighs 530 pounds.

★ Each clock face is 40 feet, 3½ inches wide.

★ Each clock face has 76 pieces of glass and weighs 2 tons.

★ The tower is 333 feet tall from the sidewalk to the top of the flagpole.

The smaller tower next to the clock tower will tell you the temperature.

The Allen Bradley Clock Tower ⇒ **stands tall above the city.**

WHAT TIME IS IT?

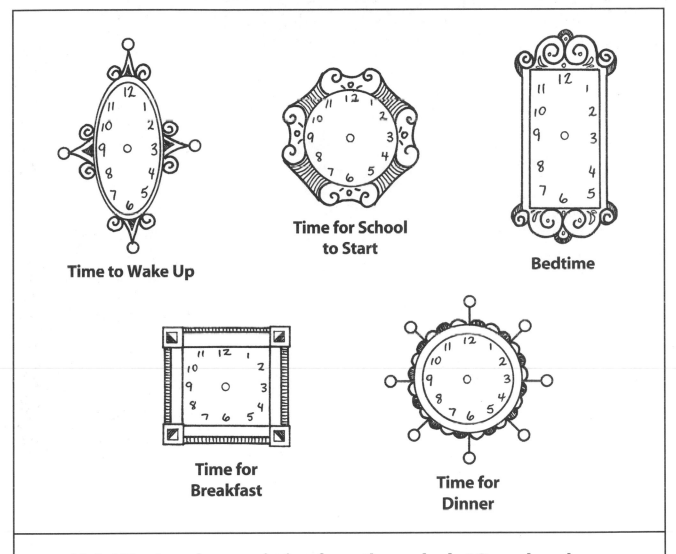

Time to Wake Up

Time for School
to Start

Bedtime

Time for
Breakfast

Time for
Dinner

**Help! The hands are missing from these clocks! Draw hands on
each one to show what time you do each of these activities.**

WAR MEMORIAL AND THE MILWAUKEE ART MUSEUM

⬆ **The War Memorial Center pays tribute to soldiers who fought for our freedom.**

The Lakefront Festival of the Arts is held outdoors next to the Milwaukee Art Museum in June.

The War Memorial Center and the Milwaukee Art Museum are two buildings that look like one. The War Memorial Center sits on legs on top of the art museum. Look at the mosaic on the War Memorial. The Roman numerals tell the years the United States fought in World War II and the Korean Conflict.

The entrance to the Milwaukee Art Museum is on the south side of the building. Inside, look for work by Andy Warhol and Picasso. If you like paintings that tell stories, visit the Von Schleinitz collection. If you like colorful art, don't miss the Haitian collection. The museum's "Family Sundays" programs let kids and parents paint, draw, build, and have fun together with art.

CREATE A PORTRAIT

Portraits are paintings or drawings of people. You'll find many portraits in most art museums. Create your own portrait of someone you're traveling with in the empty frame.

PABST MANSION

Frederick Pabst was a Great Lakes steamboat captain. After he married, he went into the brewery business.

His house is as fancy on the inside as it is on the outside. Wood carvings and paintings top each doorway. The floors and ceilings have elaborate designs, as do the chandeliers and fireplaces. When Captain Pabst gave a party, people came in carriages. Men climbed the steps to the front door. Women stepped from the carriage to the covered entry on the side. During the party, musicians played in a nook off the main hall.

The house has two safes and the study has secret hiding places. A dollhouse in an upstairs bedroom is decorated like an 1890s mansion.

The mansion's east wing was the Pabst Pavilion at the 1893 World's Columbian Exposition in Chicago.

The Pabst Mansion in all its splendor

MANSION MAZE

**It's easy to get lost in a mansion! Help these
lost kids find their way to the front door.**

NORTH POINT WATER TOWER AND THE EAST SIDE

The North Point Water Tower looks like something from a fairy tale. In fact, a Milwaukee artist created a dragon and hung it on the tower.

The tower is designed in a style called Victorian Gothic. It was built in 1873 as part of Milwaukee's water system. The tower protects a stand pipe that is no longer used. At one time, water moved up and down in the pipe to keep the pressure in the city's main water lines even.

The tower is on Milwaukee's East Side. You'll see mansions and beautiful homes in this area. **The Oriental Theater**, a real movie palace, is here, too. So is the **University of Wisconsin-Milwaukee**.

Wisconsin's famous architect, Frank Lloyd Wright, designed several Milwaukee homes, the Annunciation Greek Orthodox Church, and the Frederick C. Bogk House near the water tower.

An artist's dragon mounted on the tower inspires fairy-tale pretending. ⇝

GOOFY GARGOYLES

Gargoyles come in many shapes and sizes. Draw a line connecting the two gargoyles that match.

THE HOAN BRIDGE

If you look down the lake shore, you can't miss it. When you go to **Henry Maier Festival Park** or visit the **Port of Milwaukee**, you go under it. What is it? It's the Hoan Bridge.

The Hoan Bridge is part of Milwaukee's freeway system. For a long time it was called "The Bridge to Nowhere" because it led only to quiet city streets. People thought it should connect with another fast moving freeway. Someday it might, but for now, it's a nice shortcut from the south side of the city to downtown. If you ride over the bridge, you can see for miles over the lake and the city. Did you notice the gold arches along the bridge? They cross the entrance to the Milwaukee Harbor.

⇛

The Hoan Bridge is also called the "Harbor Bridge."

BRIDGES, BRIDGES

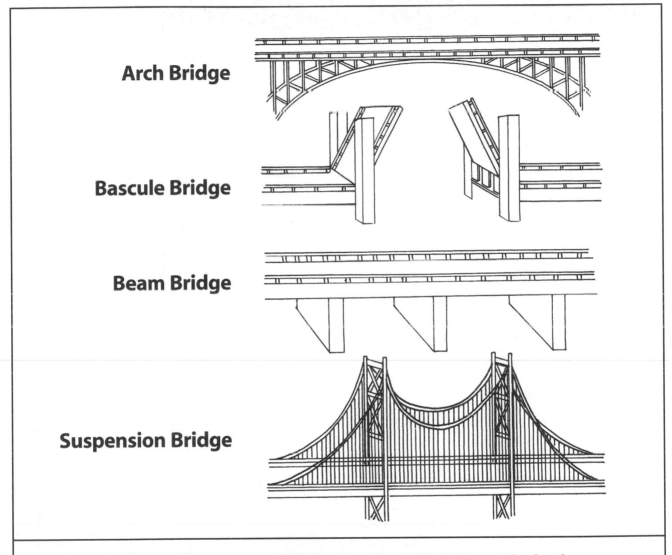

Arch Bridge

Bascule Bridge

Beam Bridge

Suspension Bridge

Here are four of the many different types of bridges. Circle the ones you have seen in Milwaukee. Then color the bridges.

GENERAL MITCHELL INTERNATIONAL AIRPORT

There is more to do at General Mitchell International Airport than catch a plane. For starters, wander around the upper level concession mall. You can count the hearts on the **Peace Mural**, titled *Clay: A Healing Way*. Stand under the 1,850-pound Calder mobile, *Red, Black and Blue*. Can you see it move? Look overhead to find the full-sized *Pteranodon*, a flying creature from the age of dinosaurs. You can even check out the double wings of the 1911 Curtiss Pusher biplane.

Have you ever wondered what an airplane's cockpit looks like? To find out, buzz into The **Mitchell Gallery of Flight**. You'll also find models of the Graf Zeppelin II airship, a Boeing 757, and military and passenger planes.

↑ **The Curtiss Pusher biplane hangs from the ceiling of General Mitchell International Airport.**

To watch planes take off and land, have your folks park in the observation lot off Layton Avenue on the north side of the airport.

AIRPORT MADNESS

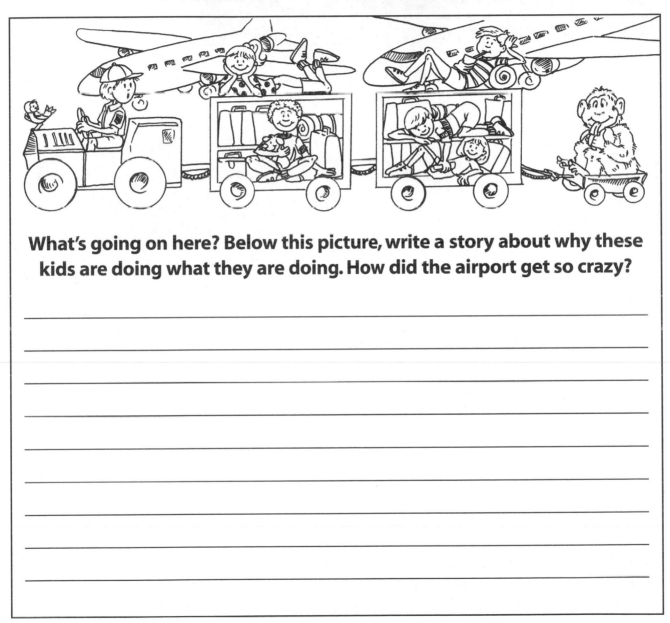

What's going on here? Below this picture, write a story about why these kids are doing what they are doing. How did the airport get so crazy?

_____

_____

_____

_____

_____

_____

_____

_____

_____

St. Joan of Arc, known for her bravery, is a French national heroine.

The St. Joan of Arc Chapel is the oldest building in the United States.

ST. JOAN OF ARC CHAPEL AT MARQUETTE UNIVERSITY

The St. Joan of Arc Chapel was built in France over 500 years ago. When the chapel was moved to the United States in 1927 it was a giant jigsaw puzzle. Each piece was marked to tell builders where it belonged. The chapel was taken apart and put together twice, first in New York, then here in Milwaukee.

St. Joan lived in France in the 1400s. She was only as tall as a fifth grader, but she led her people into battle. A stone she prayed on before battle is part of the chapel. If you touch the stone, it feels cooler than the walls around it.

Look at the floor. You'll see the tombstone of a "White Knight"—a person who fought for a good cause. The small bell near the altar was used to call people to services. People still pray here.

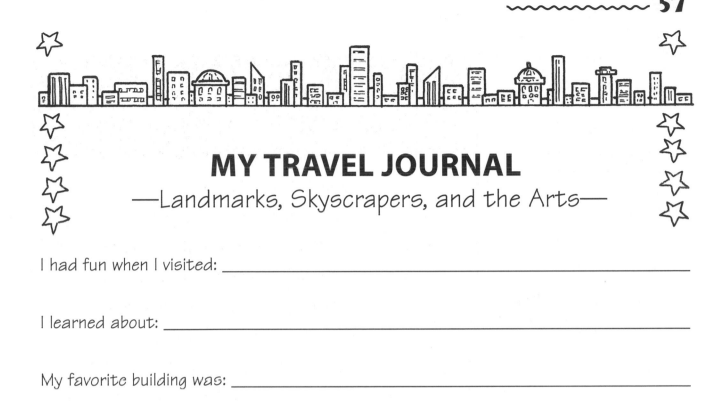

MY TRAVEL JOURNAL
—Landmarks, Skyscrapers, and the Arts—

I had fun when I visited: _____

I learned about: _____

My favorite building was: _____

This is a picture of a building I saw in Milwaukee

GOOD SPORTS

ARE YOU LOOKING FOR SPORTS ACTION? Depending on the season, you can watch major league baseball, basketball, soccer, or hockey. Teams from Marquette University and the University of Wisconsin-Milwaukee draw crowds of excited fans. The semi-pro Mustangs play arena-football at the Bradley Center. Indy and NASCAR races run at the Milwaukee Mile, while local drivers ride the track at nearby Hales Corners Speedway. On weekends, sailboats skim across the lake in races, and charter boats take people fishing on the lake.

Crowds of people come out onto the city's streets and parks for walks, runs, and bicycle races. Stables just outside the city offer horseback riding. When winter sets in, sledding, skating, and cross-country skiing are favorite activities.

⇡ **Ice hockey is also played at the Bradley Center.**

An arena-football field is 50 yards long—half the size of an NFL field.

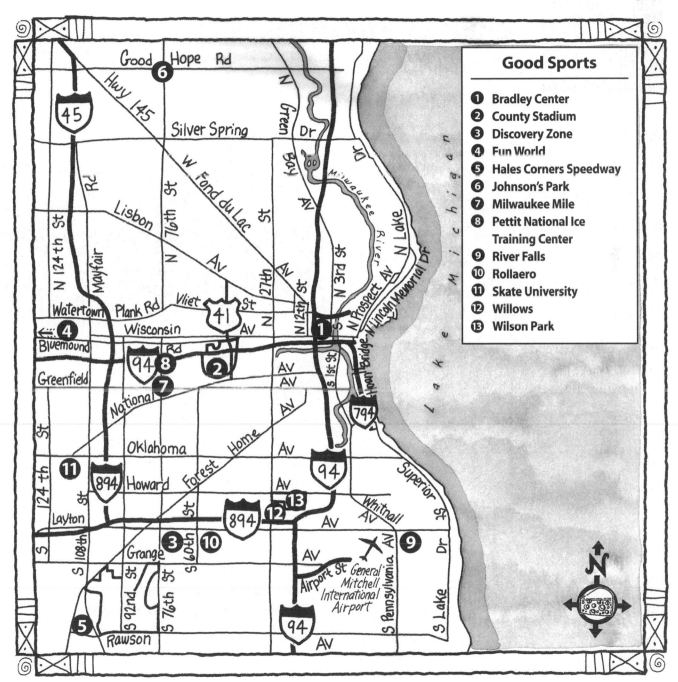

Good Sports

1. Bradley Center
2. County Stadium
3. Discovery Zone
4. Fun World
5. Hales Corners Speedway
6. Johnson's Park
7. Milwaukee Mile
8. Pettit National Ice Training Center
9. River Falls
10. Rollaero
11. Skate University
12. Willows
13. Wilson Park

MILWAUKEE BREWERS

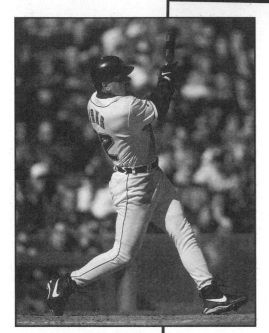

⬆ **A big swing from a Brewers player could mean a home run.**

The Milwaukee Brewers run the bases at **County Stadium**. This is where Hank Aaron hit his last home run and Robin Yount made his 3000th career hit. Two other Brewers made baseball history. Paul Moliter had the fifth-longest hitting streak in the history of baseball. Rollie Fingers was the first relief pitcher to receive the Cy Young Award and the MVP Award in the same year.

Opening Day is in April, and after a long winter without the game, many fans have "Brewers fever." They come early, set up grills, and have tailgate parties in the parking lot.

When the Brewers slam a home run, watch Bernie Brewer's house behind center field. Bernie celebrates by sliding into a giant beer mug and releasing balloon bubbles.

The Brewers' new stadium, Miller Park, is being built in part of County Stadium's parking lot.

MILWAUKEE BREWERS

Hidden in this word search are some things you might find at a baseball game. Search for words vertically, horizontally, and diagonally. Can you find all 11 words? The first word has been found for you.

Word Box		
ball	coach	pitcher
bases	diamond	strike
bat	home	umpire
catcher	plate	

```
S S A Q T I O C K A V L E F S
T B C Z T P U A R A O B I U V
R Y A S P G M T X P L A T E N
I N N L B A P C O S S T O Q U
K G Y J L F I H X G O G L M L
E D E R H A R E L Y S H Z R S
K F O C S Z E R O O L J O Q T
U D A F M U E B A S E S F M D
V O T O H O L K O H T A O R E
C O Y J S A K O J W E A B R O
N F M A D I A M O N D W E A C
J R E S T A K P I T C H E R T
```

THE MILWAUKEE BUCKS

Are you ready for some pounding NBA action? From October to April, the **Bradley Center** is the place to be.

It's game time! The Bucks bound down the court toward the basket. A guard reaches to prevent the throw. Too late—it's gone! A basket! Bango, the Bucks' mascot, waggles his antlers and does a little dance as the crowd cheers.

The first half is over. Stay where you are and the **ENERGEE** dancers will entertain you. When they're not on the floor, you'll hear the jazzy music of **Streetlife**, the Bucks' band.

There's always something going on at a Bucks game. If you can take your eyes off the players, check the scoreboard for cheers or laser light shows.

⬆ **The Milwaukee Bucks are about to score!**

The Bradley Center is also home to Marquette's NCAA Division One basketball team, the Golden Eagles.

CROSSWORD FUN

Go, Bucks! Solve this crossword by figuring out the clues of completing the sentences. If you need help, use the clue box.

Across

3. _____ is the name of the Bucks' mascot.
4. The object of basketball: get the ball through the _____.
6. This string "basket" hangs from the hoop.
7. _____life, the Bucks' band, plays jazz music.

Down

1. Basketball is played on a _____.
2. This team leader stands on the sidelines and calls the shots.
3. The Bucks play at the _____ Center.
5. A basket made from across the court scores three _____.
8. The players work together as a _____ to win the game.

THE MILWAUKEE WAVE

⇑ **A Waves game is packed wth excitement.**

↗ **Din-o-mite struts his stuff for the team.**

Sit tight and keep your eyes on the ball. The action is fast! This is Waves National Professional Soccer League Soccer. From October to March, and through the playoffs in April, watch for heading, dribbling, passing, shooting, rebounds, tackling, shoot-outs, and goals. Expect lots of offsides and penalty shots, as well.

Din-o-mite, the Wave's dinosaur mascot, takes the floor between quarters. He's seldom alone—contests for the fans are part of intermissions. At the end of half time the players and Din-o-mite toss mini soccer balls to the audience. If you catch one, hang on to it for the autograph session after the game.

Wave players come to Summerfest each day of the festival. They give soccer tips and sign autographs. They make other appearances too. Call the ticket office to find out where they'll be and when.

WHAT'S THE DIFFERENCE?

**These soccer game scenes may look alike, but they are not.
How many differences between the two scenes can you find?
Hint: There are at least 11 differences.**

THE MILWAUKEE MILE AUTO RACING

Varoom—they're off and racing for the checkered flag! The Milwaukee Mile was built in the late 1800s. It's the oldest continuously running major speedway in the United States, but things have changed since horses raced here way back then!

Each June, Indy cars roar around the flat, blacktop oval. Their speeds can average 190 mph on the straightaways. This is the Miller 200 with famous drivers like Andretti, Unser, Rahal, and Fittipaldi. NASCAR super trucks and BGN stock cars take to the oval for the Fourth of July. Cars average 130 mph on the straightaways. August brings fender-to-fender racing with the American Speed Association's "Badgerland 150." The competition is fierce!

NASCAR racers Dick Trickle and Dave Marcis are from Wisconsin.

There's nonstop action at the Milwaukee Mile.

SILLY STORY

Without telling anyone what you're doing, ask for a word to fill in each blank. For example, "Give me an action word." When all the blanks are filled in, read the story out loud. One of the blanks has been filled in for you.

It was the day before the big race. Alex and Tim were __laugh__ing
<u>action word</u>

in the pit area inside the racetrack. Crews and drivers were working

on their cars. "_____!" said Alex. "There's_____. He's won
<u>exclamation</u>   <u>name 1</u>

_____ races this year." The boys ran over to look at his car.
<u>number</u>

"This sure is a _____ car," Alex said. "Thanks," said
<u>describing word</u>

_____. "I'm taking it on a test run around the track in a few
<u>name 1</u>

minutes. How about a ride?" The boys looked at each other in

_____. Tim looked into the car. "Sure," he said. "But where do we
<u>emotion</u>

sit? There's only one seat." "No problem," said _____. "You can
<u>name 1</u>

ride on the _____."
<u>thing</u>

PETTIT NATIONAL ICE TRAINING CENTER

The winter Olympics are alive in Milwaukee all year, every year. Milwaukee's Pettit National Ice Training Center is an official U.S. Olympic Training Site. The huge building has two international-size ice-skating rinks and a speed skaters' oval. Only five buildings like this exist in the world. This is the only one in the United States.

Members of the U.S. Speedskating Team usually train mornings and evenings. You can watch their practices, and you might see Olympic medal-winners like Bonnie Blair and Dan Jansen. They're retired, but they still like to skate.

Local skating clubs and hockey teams skate here, too. Call to find out when the rink is open to the public. The center rents skates and gives lessons.

⇡ *The Skater* is a sculpture outside of the Pettit National Ice Training Center.

Casey FitzRandolph, the 1996 U.S. Men's Sprint Champion, and Chris Witty, the 1996 U.S. Ladies Sprint Champion, practice at the Pettit National Ice Center.

HIDE AND SEEK

**There are 12 objects hidden in this ice rink scene.
Can you find them all? Look for: lamp, mug, cup, fork, pencil,
bell, baseball bat, turtle, snake, bone, toothbrush, and paintbrush.**

SPORTS FOR YOU

⬆ **Don't forget your jacket—even indoor ice-skating can be a chilly experience.**

Many Milwaukee County Parks have fitness trails. Do the exercises at each station for a complete workout.

Tennis courts, bike paths, and hiking trails are scattered throughout the city. If you would like to ride a horse, check a local phone book's yellow pages for a list of stables.

For indoor roller-skating, try **Rollaero** or **Skate University**. If ice-skating is your thing, **Wilson Park** and the **Pettit Center** have ice all year-round. For more indoor fun, try **Fun World**. This place is huge! Check out the Ferris wheel, air hockey, mini golf, video games, and laser tag. If tubes, slides, bridges, and ball pits are more your style, try **DZ**, the **Discovery Zone**.

Willows and **River Falls** are good spots for miniature golf, and both places have batting cages. Another place, **Johnson's Park**, has go-carts.

MY TRAVEL JOURNAL
—Good Sports—

I had fun when I visited: _____

I learned about: _____

My favorite sport is: _____

I like it because: _____

This is a picture of my favorite sport

6 MUSEUMS AND MORE

DO YOU HAVE QUESTIONS? MUSEUMS CAN GIVE you answers and teach you about the world.

How did firemen fight fires before there were hydrants? They pumped water from rivers, ponds, or wells using special trucks and hoses. The Milwaukee County Historical Center has a pumper truck built in the 1860s, a collection of toys from the 1800s, and scenes from a nineteenth-century drug store and bank.

What does an Excalibur look like? You'll know if you stroll through the Brooks Stevens Automobile Collection. You'll see luxury cars, antique cars, early racing cars, and sports cars.

There are many different kinds of museums. They're great places to take your questions and your imagination.

An old-fashioned drug store at the Milwaukee County Historical Center

Learn about stars and planets at the Olsen Planetarium on the University of Wisconsin–Milwaukee campus.

Museums and More

❶ Betty Brinn Children's Museum
❷ Brooks Stevens Automobile Collection
❸ Discovery World
❹ International Clown Hall of Fame
❺ Milwaukee County Historical Center
❻ Milwaukee Maritime Center & Wisconsin Lake Schooner Education Association
❼ Milwaukee Public Museum
❽ Old World Wisconsin
❾ Scout Heritage Museum

MILWAUKEE PUBLIC MUSEUM

At the Milwaukee Public Museum you can travel through time and go around the world.

Start with the Third Planet exhibit's dinosaur hall. Are you ready for the roar of the Tyrannosaurus?

Next proceed to the rain forest exhibit. You won't need an umbrella. When you're done, move on to the model European village. Walk the cobblestone streets of Old Milwaukee, then watch a nickelodeon movie.

The Egyptian exhibit shines with golden splendor. These temples, mounds, and tombs hold mummies! Safari through Africa, or plunge into the ocean. Visit a noisy marketplace in South America or India, or see how North American Indians lived and hunted.

Visit the museum on Saturdays and Sundays at 1 p.m. and you can try crafts, play games, or go on scavenger hunts during the "Afternoon Adventures" program.

↑ **The Milwaukee Public Museum**

The dinosaur skull at the museum is the world's largest. It's a *Torosaurus.*

CONNECT THE DOTS

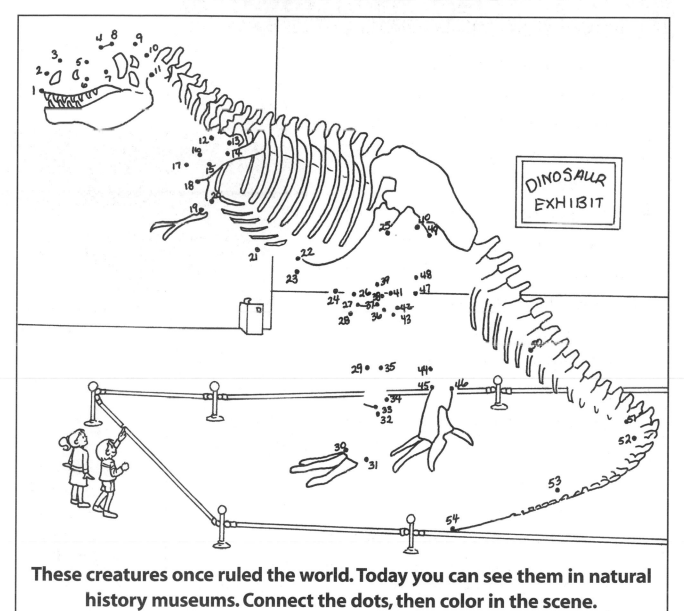

These creatures once ruled the world. Today you can see them in natural history museums. Connect the dots, then color in the scene.

THE INTERNATIONAL CLOWN HALL OF FAME

Get your face painted at the International Clown Hall of Fame.

Floppy feet and red noses are popular at the International Clown Hall of Fame. The Hall of Fame features real clowns as well as pictures and exhibits.

The exhibits honor 39 clowns from all over the world. Visitors learn how the different clowns dressed and what they did to make people laugh.

Not all clowns wear white makeup and big smiles! Emmett Kelly wore a sad face and he's one of the world's most famous clowns.

You can look around by yourself or take a tour of the Hall of Fame. If you take the tour, you might learn a few clowning tricks or get your face painted. You'll definitely see a live performance. Maybe you'll even be in it!

A clown shapes balloons in front of an eager audience.

The Ringling Bros. Circus is famous around the world. It's one of more than 100 circuses that started in Wisconsin.

CLOWNING AROUND

Two of the clowns in this circus are exactly the same. When you find these two clowns draw a circle around each one of them.

THE BETTY BRINN CHILDREN'S MUSEUM

Do you like to pretend? Would you like to be a farmer with a vegetable stand, a cook at a restaurant, or a teller at a bank? Or would you rather drive an ambulance?

At the Betty Brinn Children's Museum you can be all those and more.

The idea here is to learn while you play, and the choices seem endless. You can walk through a giant heart and follow the path of a blood cell, or travel though a giant ear and follow the path of a sound wave. Try your navigating skills on a wheelchair course. Other attractions include fun-house mirrors, a toy-making craft center, and a weaving corner. There's even an area for little kids called **The Play Port.**

⇧ **Don't eat the apples on this tree at the Betty Brinn Children's Museum!**

The Betty Brinn Children's Museum is named to honor a Milwaukee woman who tried to make life better for abused and neglected children.

ADVENTURE AT THE BETTY BRINN

Without telling anyone what you're doing, ask for a word to fill in each blank. For example, "Give me an action word." When all the blanks are filled in, read the story out loud. One blank has been filled in for you.

Maria and Jon were having a great time at the museum. "That

was ___curly___," said Jon after they _____ed through the
    describing word   action word

wheelchair course. "What do you want to do next?" "It's hard to

decide," said Maria. "There are _____ things we haven't tried
                   number

yet." "I'm going to pretend I'm a farmer," said Jon. "You can come

visit my vegetable stand." "OK," agreed Maria, "I'll buy a _____
                                    describing word

_____." "What will you do with that?" Jon asked. "I'll take it
vegetable

to the craft center," said Maria. "And _____ it into a toy
                           action word

_____!"
thing

DISCOVERY WORLD

You probably know how a teeter-totter works. Did you know you can use the same idea to lift a boulder? A display in Discovery World tells you how and lets you do it. The section on levers, gears, and pulleys shows that a little strength can do a lot of work.

You can do and learn about plenty of other things in this hands-on museum. You can see how X-rays work and learn how magnets make electricity—it's an "en-light-ening" experience. You can surf the Internet or visit the **R&D Cafe**, which serves up experiments like making paper. "Family Fusion" workshops use common things like cabbage juice and ice cream to explore scientific ideas. Special shows include **"Electro, a Show of Electricity,"** and **"Light Waves and Laser Beams."**

⬆ **The Van de Graaf generator's electricity will make your stand on end.**

Gears, levers, pulleys, and electricity play an important role in Milwaukee manufacturing.

HIDDEN MESSAGE

Do you know who discovered the electric lightbulb?

The answer is hidden in the box below. To find it, cross out all the X's, Y's, K's, F's, G's, W's, J's and Q's. The letters remaining spell the answer to this riddle!

X	T	Y	F	K	H	K	O	Q	F	X	F	J	W	Q	G	J
W	K	X	M	K	G	W	F	X	A	G	S	K	W	Y	F	G
K	A	Y	K	L	X	K	J	J	F	Y	X	V	Q	Y	X	W
W	A	J	F	K	X	F	E	J	K	Y	G	Y	G	X	Y	X
J	Y	W	D	X	I	G	X	Y	X	G	F	S	K	F	G	W
G	X	Y	X	X	O	F	W	F	K	G	X	Y	N	Y	G	K

Write the hidden message here:

_____

THE SCOUT HERITAGE MUSEUM

⚜ **The Boy Scouts have been around since 1908.**

The museum is in the Milwaukee County Scout Council's headquarters. Craft kits and scouting gear are for sale.

Perhaps you or someone you know is a Boy Scout. Milwaukee's Scout Heritage Museum is a one-room museum that's packed full of scouting memorabilia. You have to look carefully to take it all in!

One display holds badges from different countries. Another has merit badges earned by U.S. Scouts from 1933 to present-day. And don't forget to look up. Scout hats sit above a sampling of uniforms from 1911 to the present. You won't believe the neckerchief slides! Postcards show scout uniforms from around the world.

Check corners of the museum to find the stone ax that is over 100 years old. A display on *The Order of the Arrow* is tucked away, too.

Ben Hunt, a Milwaukee-area scoutmaster, made the drum, Indian head-dress, totem pole, and buckskin clothing. A full-sized canoe based on his model stands outside the museum.

BOY SCOUT HERITAGE

Hidden in this word search are some things you might see at the Heritage Scout Museum. Search for words vertically, horizontally, and diagonally. Can you find all 11 words? The first word has been found for you.

Word Box

badges	drum	headdress
neckerchief	totem pole	buckskin
ax	canoe	uniform
hats	postcards	

```
A M N E C K E R C H I E F H A
T C O N F R E A B L S A S B P
O A B O F G C R B U B K O P O
T K D A L J A S T N A M O S S
E F X K D T N K T I A P E Z T
M G A F S G O E L F H A T S C
P V Z O B S E T C O Z F M A A
O W J A A K B S T R E U X J R
L B U C K S K I N M R U Y H D
E A Q U M I S T L D A I Z O S
O L A A D L B C E R E P G B A
E T X C W H E A D D R E S S L
```

WISCONSIN LAKE SCHOONER EDUCATION ASSOCIATION

Schooners with billowing sails once cut through the waves on Lake Michigan. Passengers were headed for the frontier villages that grew into the cities we know today.

The Lake Schooner Education Association is building a schooner like the ones that sailed in the 1800s. When it's finished, students from grade school through college will sail on it. They'll learn about sailing and use the boat to do research projects. The ship will be launched during Wisconsin's 150th birthday year, 1998. You can watch it being built Tuesday through Saturday on the grounds of the **Milwaukee Maritime Center**.

A student adjusts a mast on a schooner at the Wisconsin Lake Schooner Education Association.

The schooner's masts are made from the timber of a 160-year-old white pine. The tree sprouted before Wisconsin became a state.

CONNECT THE DOTS

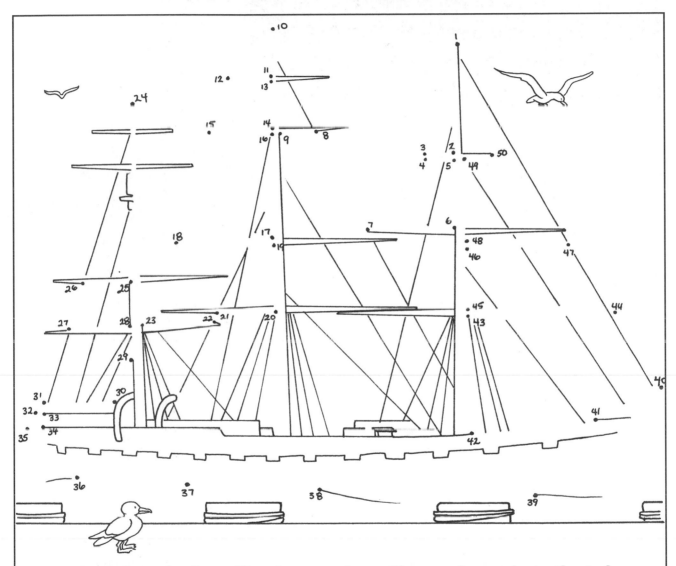

You might see a boat like the one above if you take a trip to the Lake Schooner Education Association. Connect the dots, then color in the scene.

OLD WORLD WISCONSIN

Visiting Old World Wisconsin is like traveling back in time. Farm work is done by hand with the help of horses. Candles and lanterns are used for light when it's needed. Cookstoves and fireplaces are used for cooking. You feel as if you are back in the 1800s, when Wisconsin was being settled. The people in the buildings are dressed as if they lived back then. You can visit them while they make bread, feed the animals, or spin flax.

Ethnic Crossroads Village in Old World Wisconsin has an inn, general store, church, town hall, and blacksmith shop. Beyond the village are ethnic farms. Each of the buildings was brought here from somewhere in Wisconsin. Even the outhouses were built and used by early settlers.

⬆ **Step back in time at Old World Wisconsin.**

Raspberry School has one room, and there's no house for the teacher. She stayed in the homes of her students and their families!

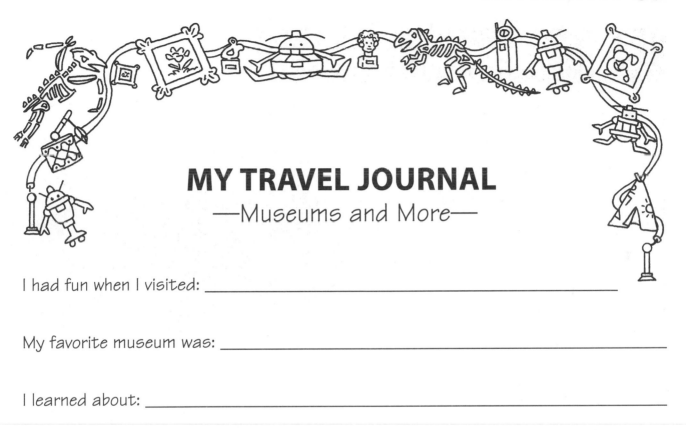

MY TRAVEL JOURNAL
—Museums and More—

I had fun when I visited: _____

My favorite museum was: _____

I learned about: _____

This is a picture of an exhibit I saw in Milwaukee

7 THAT'S ENTERTAINMENT

LOOKING FOR SOME FUN? CHECK THE "CUE" section of the *Milwaukee Journal Sentinel*, or look through the *Milwaukee Magazine*. *Curiocity*, a newspaper for kids, lists entertainment, too. The Milwaukee Parks Special Event Line gives park activities.

There are many things to do in Milwaukee. Wisconsin State Fair Park has craft, horse, dog, and model railroading shows; Western Days has a rodeo; and, of course, there's the Wisconsin State Fair. The Wisconsin Center hosts local events like the Holiday Folk Fair, and national shows like Holiday on Ice. Henry Maier Festival Park has festivals all summer. Milwaukee's many theaters present concerts, plays, and ballet, and there are over 30 movie theaters and many shopping centers.

⤊ **Henry Maier Festival Park**

Check the Calendar and Resource Guide at the back of this book for more entertainment ideas.

That's Entertainment

1. **Audubon Court Books**
2. **Avalon Theatre**
3. **Book Bay Children's Books**
4. **Cool Waters**
5. **Grand Avenue Mall**
6. **Harry W. Schwartz Booksellers**
7. **Humbolt Park Bandshell**
8. **Iroquois Harbor Cruises**
9. **Renaissance Book Shop**
10. **Washington Park Bandshell**
11. **West Allis Farmers' Market**
12. **Wisconsin Center**
13. **Wisconsin State Fair Park**

GRAND AVENUE MALL

⬆ **The circular stairway in the Plankinton Building is unique.**

The skywalk over the Milwaukee River is the only skywalk in the U.S. that spans a river used by boats.

Shopping in a place like the Grand Avenue is fun. This downtown mall is really five buildings connected by two skywalks. If you stand in the skywalk you can watch cars drive under you.

There are interesting things to do in both the old and the new sections. The **Plankinton Building**, the oldest part, was built in 1915. Peek over the fancy ironwork of the circular staircase to see the fountain on the lowest level. The food court is on the top floor of the newest section. Before you go up, watch the mechanical bear. He rides a unicycle back and forth on the tightrope over the reflecting pool.

WHICH ARE THE SAME?

Two of these unicycle-riding bears are identical.
Can you find which two are the same?

IROQUOIS HARBOR CRUISES

⬆ The *Iroquois* heads for adventure on the Milwaukee River.

Alewives are small fish that don't taste good. They came to Lake Michigan through the St. Lawrence Seaway.

Ahoy Mates! If you're ready for a watery adventure, board the *Iroquois* for a cruise.

The *Iroquois* captain, Captain Blackheart, knows the river's twists and turns. He pilots his boat down the Milwaukee River past houseboats, sailboats, and pleasure crafts. He heads for that big puddle, Lake Michigan.

Keep sharp! The Captain's questions will catch you if you're not listening. There's plenty to see and the Captain sees it all. Did that fishing boat take on alewives or perch? Are those tugs headed into harbor or out? What's being loaded into that freighter's hatch?

Keep your eyes and your ears tuned! You'll see and hear as much as the Captain!

WHAT'S THE DIFFERENCE?

These two harbor scenes may look the same, but they're not. Can you find at least 14 differences between the two pictures? After you are done, color the scene.

COOL WATERS AT GREENFIELD PARK

You'll be all wet when you come to Cool Waters to play! This family aquatic center offers wading and regular swimming pools, water activities and slides, a picnic area, and sand volleyball courts.

Grab a tube, then twist and turn down the slide to the splash pool. Would you rather not use a tube? That is a separate slide all together!

Cool Waters also has a zero-depth pool. When you wade into this pool it feels like you're walking into a lake or an ocean. The pool slopes gradually from a depth of "0" feet to a depth of 5 feet. First your feet get wet, then your ankles. The water gets deeper until you're at the far end of the pool where the swimming lanes are located.

The water mushrooms and jet sprays are in the shallow water. So is the "Lily Pad Walk." Will you make it across? Hang on to the rope. If you lose your balance, you're in the drink!

⇑ **The Cool Waters logo is a water drop named "Cool."**

Water cools you off on a hot day because it takes heat from your skin and carries it away.

SUMMER FUN AT COOL WATERS

Without telling anyone what you're doing, ask for a word to fill in each blank. For example, "Give me an action word." When all the blanks are filled in, read the story out loud. One blank has been filled in for you.

Leslie and _____ were __happy__ ! They were spending the
           name 1   emotion

whole day at Cool Waters. "I can't wait to _____ down the
                            action word

water slide," said Leslie. "Me too," agreed _____, "but first let's
                                    name 1

try the Lily Pad Walk." They raced to the pool and _____ed
                                     action word

onto the first lily pad. Halfway across Leslie lost her balance and

fell into the water. "_____!" said Leslie. "This isn't as
                Exclamation

_____ as it looks. Hang onto the _____, or just pretend
describing word   thing

you're a _____ and _____ from pad to pad."
         animal   action word

BOOKSTORES

Did you know that authors Lois Ehlert, Kevin Henkes, Laura Ingalls Wilder, and Betty Ren Wright are from Wisconsin? The people at **Book Bay Children's Books** do, and they can name other Wisconsin authors and illustrators, too. Check out their special section of autographed books. They may have something signed by your favorite author.

⇑ **Authors often read books to kids at the Harry W. Schwartz Bookshops.**

Another bookstore, **Audubon Court Books**, has big soft chairs. You can sit down and look at the books before you buy them. Before you leave, your folks may want to have coffee in the store's café.

There are four **Harry W. Schwartz Bookshops** around Milwaukee. Some are near malls, so book buying can be easy when you're shopping. All of these bookstores have story hours and children's programs. Sometimes authors come in to sign books. Call to find out what's planned so you can try to be there.

The Renaissance Book Shop sells used books. Shopping here is like going on a treasure hunt.

BOOKWORM MANIA

START

FINISH

This bookworm is trying to get to a reading chair.
Can you help him find a path?

WEST ALLIS FARMERS' MARKET

⇑ **A farmer displays his vegetables at the Farmers' Market.**

The West Allis Farmers' Market is almost 70 years old. A farmer donated the land for the market in the 1920s.

Wisconsin farmers grow a lot of different things, and one place they sell them is the West Allis Farmer's Market. Selling and buying at the farmers' market is a family activity Tuesday, Thursday, and Saturday afternoons from May to November.

In spring, farmers bring flowers and vegetable plants. As the weather warms up, they come with lettuce, strawberries, asparagus, spinach, beets, and peas. Summer crops include raspberries, beans, corn, green peppers, and tomatoes. Fall is the time for cauliflower, cabbage, brussels sprouts, potatoes, squash, apples, and pumpkins. Eggs, honey, and spices are sold in all seasons. The market is only open in the afternoon because everything is picked in the morning and sold fresh.

GLORIOUS FOOD

Hidden in this word search are some things you might find at a Farmers' Market. Search for words vertically, horizontally, and diagonally. Can you find all 10 words? The first word has been found for you.

Word Box

apples	cider	squash
beans	lettuce	tomato
blueberries	potato	
carrots	raspberries	

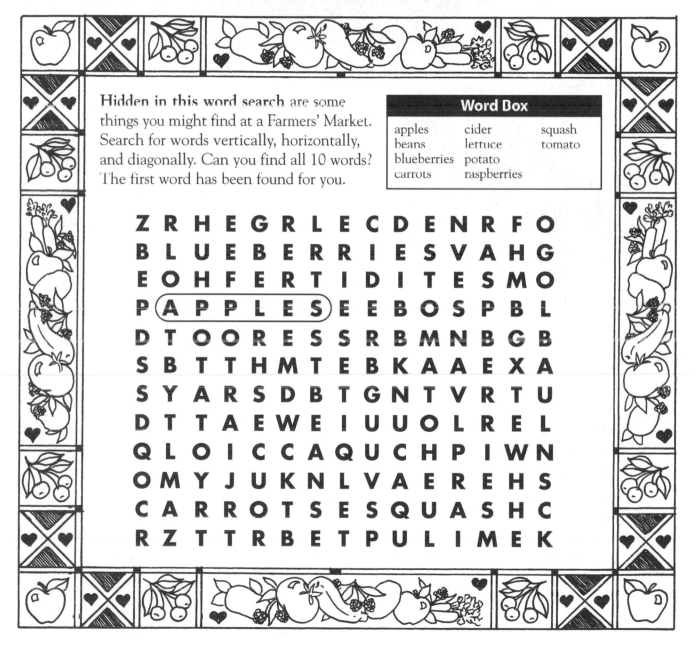

```
Z R H E G R L E C D E N R F O
B L U E B E R R I E S V A H G
E O H F E R T I D I T E S M O
P (A P P L E S) E E B O S P B L
D T O O R E S S R B M N B G B
S B T T H M T E B K A A E X A
S Y A R S D B T G N T V R T U
D T T A E W E I U U O L R E L
Q L O I C C A Q U C H P I W N
O M Y J U K N L V A E R E H S
C A R R O T S E S Q U A S H C
R Z T T R B E T P U L I M E K
```

CHILDREN'S THEATER

Do you like plays? Milwaukee has several theater companies that put on plays for children.

First Stage Milwaukee often does plays based on well-known children's stories. In the past they've done *Ramona Quimbly* and *Peter Pan*. They do several plays between September and June. Folk tales, fairy tales, and other classic stories are the specialty of **M & W Productions**. Their plays are presented in October, December, and May. Past plays have included *The Wizard of Oz* and *Rumpelstiltskin*.

The **Avalon Arts Coalition** is a group of theater companies. Its members are the **Milwaukee Youth Theater**, the **Polaris Puppet Theater**, **Milwaukee Public Theater**, the **African American Children's Theater**, and **Red Nose Productions**. They present their productions at the **Avalon Theater** from September through May.

First Stage Milwaukee in the midst of one of its many performances.

If you have orchestra seats, you won't be sitting with the musicians. The front seats are called orchestra seats.

HIDE AND SEEK!

There are 15 objects hidden in this theater scene. Can you find them all?
Look for: a bone, cup, beach ball, spool of thread, bird, tire, heart, mushroom, book, sucker, crayon, doorknob, pencil, carrot, and umbrella.

LISTEN TO THE MUSIC!

If you love music you've come to the right city. Milwaukee's summer festivals are alive with music.

RiverSplash and **Rainbow Summer** turn the Riverwalk and Peck Pavilion into rhythm centers. You can sit under the stars for **Concerts in the Park**— they're given at bandshells in Washington and Humboldt Parks, and every concert is different. There's dancing, too. The **Ko Thi Dance Company** steps to the beat of African drums. The **City Ballet Theater** presents tip-toe grace.

When winter comes, performances can be more formal. Not the **Festival City Symphony "Pajama Jamaborees,"** though! Kids come to performances in their pajamas. Every year at Christmas time the **Milwaukee Ballet** puts on *"The Nutcracker."* After Christmas, the **Milwaukee Symphony Orchestra** presents concerts for kids, called **Kinderkonzerts**.

⇑ **These young Ko-Thi Dance Company dancers would impress anyone.**

The lyre on top of the Pabst Theater represents music. The two vases represent abundance.

MY TRAVEL JOURNAL
—That's Entertainment—

These are the names of the places I visited: _____

My favorite place was: _____

The strangest thing I saw was: _____

This is a picture of something I saw in Milwaukee

8 LET'S EAT!

MILWAUKEE'S FAVORITE FOODS INCLUDE bratwurst, fried fish, frozen custard, and anything with cheese on it. You probably won't have trouble finding your favorite food here. There are Italian, German, French, Greek, Asian, and Mexican restaurants. American favorites like hamburgers and hot dogs are easy to find, and the pizza is good here, too. Many restaurants have children's menus and some serve breakfast all day.

Milwaukee has fancy restaurants as well as casual, inexpensive places. But you don't have to eat in a restaurant. Pick up some food at a grocery store deli or go to a custard stand and ask for take-out. Then head for a park and have a picnic!

⇡ **Mader's German restaurant looks like a castle from Germany.**

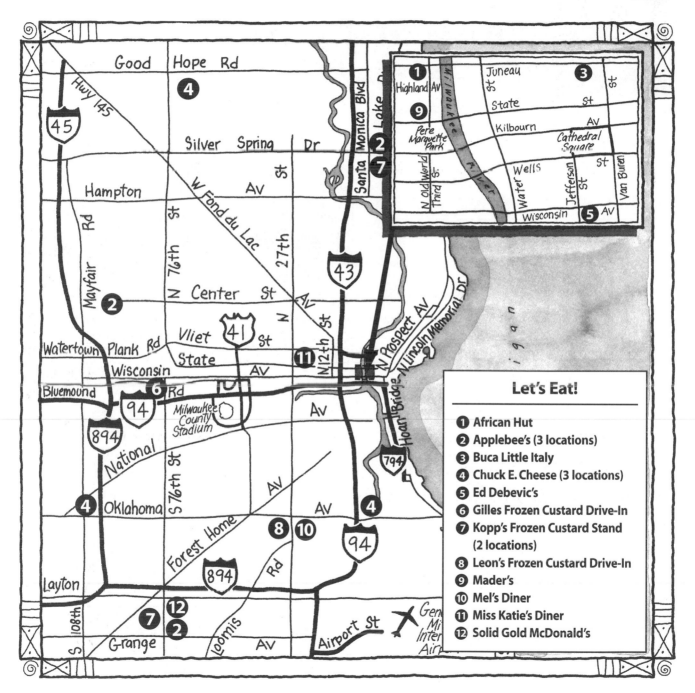

Let's Eat!

1. African Hut
2. Applebee's (3 locations)
3. Buca Little Italy
4. Chuck E. Cheese (3 locations)
5. Ed Debevic's
6. Gilles Frozen Custard Drive-In
7. Kopp's Frozen Custard Stand (2 locations)
8. Leon's Frozen Custard Drive-In
9. Mader's
10. Mel's Diner
11. Miss Katie's Diner
12. Solid Gold McDonald's

ETHNIC RESTAURANTS

If you want a meal to remember, try one of Milwaukee's ethnic restaurants.

For German foods like schnitzel and sauerbraten, visit **Mader's**. Mader's looks like a castle on the outside, and inside it's decorated with armor. The stained glass windows make everything glow.

At the **African Hut**, peanut stew and zanzi-fries are favorites. Stop in for a snack or a meal. If you want to taste something before you order, ask for a sample. You'll like the music and the leopard skin design on the wallpaper.

Music and decorations make everybody feel Italian at **Buca Little Italy**. Order pasta by the pound and you'll have enough to feed your whole family. Buca doesn't open until 5 p.m., so spend the day getting hungry.

⬆ **The African Hut serves food from Africa, of course!**

The Milwaukee Yellow Pages lists over 150 ethnic restaurants. The largest number are Chinese, but there are lots of Italian and Mexican places, too.

FIND THE FOOD

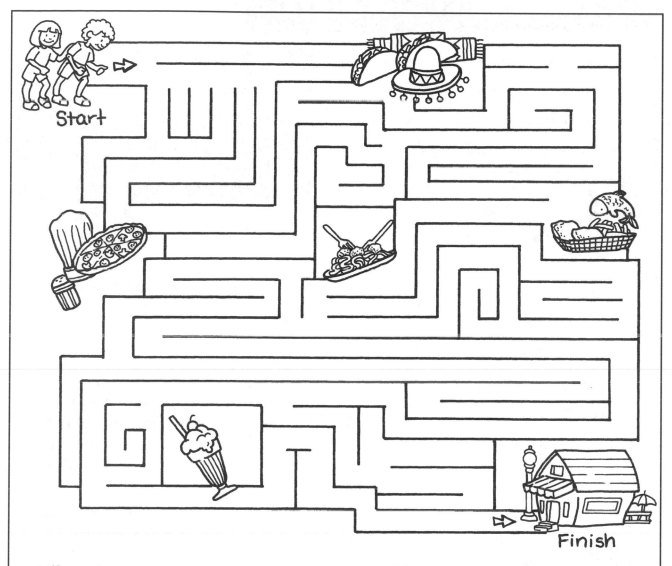

Milwaukee restaurants serve many types of food . As you wind your way through the maze, see if you can collect every kind of food that is pictured.

FOOD AND FUN

Why not have a little fun while you eat?

At **Chuck E. Cheese** you can watch the stage show and eat pizza, salad, or sandwiches. When you're done you can run through the maze or play games.

The menu at the **Solid Gold McDonald's** offers the usual "golden arches" fare. Pictures, records, posters, and articles about rock stars decorate the walls and booths. Sit on a motorcycle seat to eat at the counter. Check out the figure in the black leather jacket near the motorcycle. If you're there long enough, you'll hear the bike roar!

If you like to watch sports while you eat, you'll love **Applebee's**. Sports equipment covers the walls and the televisions are always tuned to action-packed sports events.

⚑ **Solid Gold McDonald's has a lot more than just cheeseburgers and french fries.**

Wisconsin is a dairy state and the people here love cheese. The yellow cheese called Colby was created in Colby, Wisconsin.

CHEESE, PLEASE

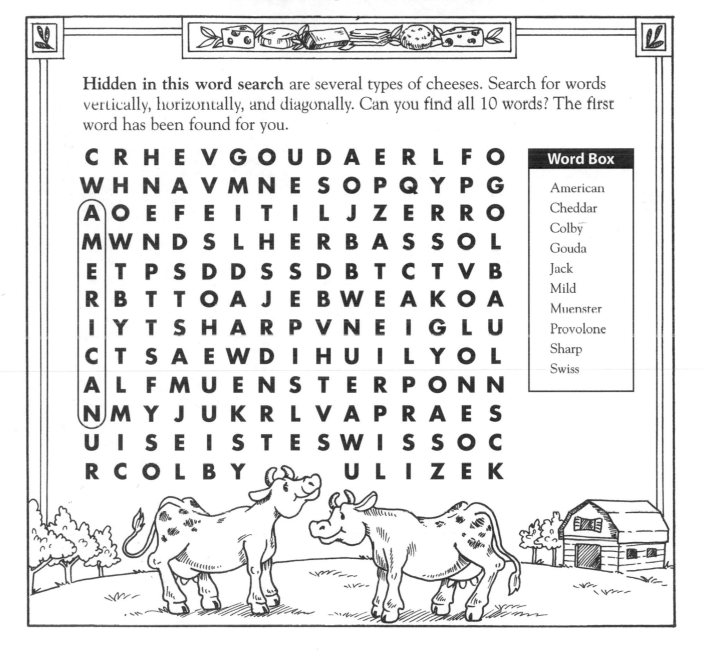

Hidden in this word search are several types of cheeses. Search for words vertically, horizontally, and diagonally. Can you find all 10 words? The first word has been found for you.

```
C R H E V G O U D A E R L F O
W H N A V M N E S O P Q Y P G
A O E F E I T I L J Z E R R O
M W N D S L H E R B A S S O L
E T P S D D S S D B T C T V B
R B T T O A J E B W E A K O A
I Y T S H A R P V N E I G L U
C T S A E W D I H U I L Y O L
A L F M U E N S T E R P O N N
N M Y J U K R L V A P R A E S
U I S E I S T E S W I S S O C
R C O L B Y       U L I Z E K
```

Word Box

- American
- Cheddar
- Colby
- Gouda
- Jack
- Mild
- Muenster
- Provolone
- Sharp
- Swiss

DINERS AND 50s ATMOSPHERE

Diners were popular places to hang out in the 1950s and 1960s. These casual restaurants serve American favorites like grilled cheese, hot dogs, hamburgers, fries, malts, and floats. Rock 'n' roll "oldies" add to the old-time atmosphere.

When President Clinton came to Milwaukee, he ate at **Miss Katie's Diner**. Ask the waitress to point out his table. The malts here are thick, and big enough to share.

Order a kid's meal at **Mel's Diner** and you'll get lunch (or dinner) in a cardboard convertible. If you've never tasted a "Black Cow," ask for one here!

There's always something happening at **Ed Debevic's**. Waiters and waitresses here tease everybody. They steal french fries off your plate and spin hula hoops. With all that's going on around you, don't forget to eat!

↑ **Miss Katie's Diner serves America's favorite— hamburgers and fries.**

Rock stars like Elvis Presley and Bill Haley and the Comets made 50s music "Shake, Rattle and Roll."

CONNECT THE DOTS

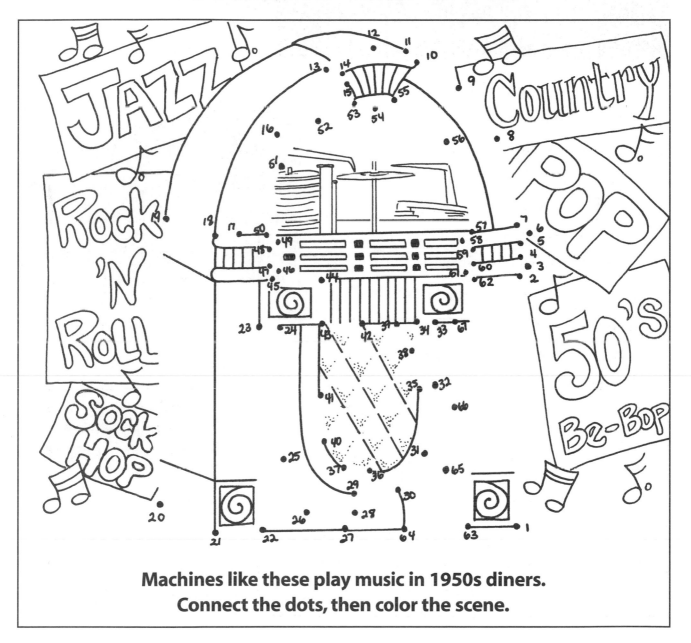

**Machines like these play music in 1950s diners.
Connect the dots, then color the scene.**

CUSTARD STANDS

Go to a custard stand for great cones, sundaes, and malts. Custard comes in three flavors: vanilla, chocolate, and the special of the day. If you want something other than dessert, you can usually order hamburgers and fries.

Gilles was the first custard stand in Milwaukee. It's been around long enough to be the grandfather of the rest. For custard on the go, **Leon's** is a neon wonder at night. But even during the day, it's fun to go to a real drive-in. No inside seating here! You could also try **Kopp's** custard—it's terrific! Their huge hamburgers were voted the best in town. When you order one, you'd better be really hungry.

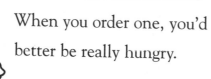

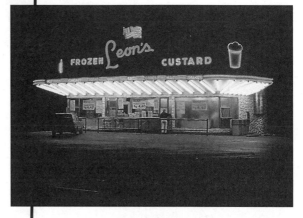

Leon's Frozen Custard lights up at night.

Custard is a creamy version of ice cream. While ice cream is made with milk, custard is made with egg yolks and thick cream.

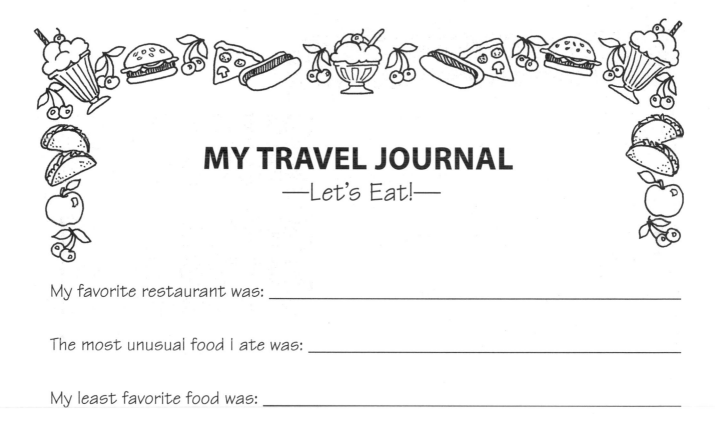

MY TRAVEL JOURNAL
—Let's Eat!—

My favorite restaurant was: _____

The most unusual food I ate was: _____

My least favorite food was: _____

This is a picture of one restaurant I visited

CALENDAR OF MILWAUKEE EVENTS

January

Firstar Day
Different locations in Milwaukee County,
(414) 765-6500
Special events celebrate New Year's Day.

Annual U.S. International Snow Sculpting Competition
Marcus Center for the Performing Arts,
(414) 272-5235

February

Milwaukee Boat Show
The Wisconsin Center, (414) 271-4000

March

Maple Sugar Weekend
Wehr Nature Center in Whitnall Park,
(414) 425-8550

April

Milwaukee Brewers Opening Day
Milwaukee County Stadium, Tickets,
(414) 933-9000

May

Miller Genuine Draft 200 Race
The Milwaukee Mile, Tickets, (414) 453-8277
Indy Car racing.

June

RiverSplash
Wisconsin Ave. to the Pleasant St. Bridge,
(414) 286-5700

West Allis Western Days
Wisconsin State Fair Park, (414) 821-7816

Rainbow Summer
Peck Pavilion of the Marcus Center for the
Performing Arts, (414)273-7206 or (800)472-4458

Lakefront Festival of Arts
Milwaukee Art Museum, (414) 224-3850

The Milwaukee Journal Sentinel Rose Festival
Boerner Botanical Gardens, (414) 529-1870
This nine day event includes daily concerts, craft

demonstrations, workshops, ethnic dancing, lectures, children's programs, and 50,000 roses in bloom.

Polish Fest
Henry Maier Festival Park, (414) 529-2140

Summerfest
Henry Maier Festival Park, (414) 273-FEST or (800)837-FEST

July

Firstar Fireworks on July 3rd
Milwaukee's lakefront, (414) 765-4321

NASCAR Sears Auto Center Motorsports Weekend
The Milwaukee Mile, Tickets, (414) 453-8277
NASCAR super trucks and BGN stock cars race during the Fourth of July weekend.

The Great Circus Parade Week
Downtown Milwaukee, (414) 273-7877

Bastille Days
East Town, Jefferson Street and Cathedral Square, (414) 271-1416
French food and displays are only part of this weekend celebration. There's a 5-K run and bicycle race, plus four stages with entertainment.

Festa Italiana
Henry Maier Festival Park, (414) 223-2180 or (414) 223-2194

Wisconsin Avenue Farmer's Market
North 4th Street and West Wisconsin Ave., (414) 543-2052

German Fest
Henry Maier Festival Park, (414) 464-9444 or (800)355-9067

Prairie Days, "A Journey Back to the TallGrass"
Wehr Nature Center, (414) 425-8550
Visitors experience life on the prairie in the 1800s through activities, crafts, history, and food.

August

Irish Fest
Henry Maier Festival Park, (414) 476-3378

Mexican Fiesta
Henry Maier Festival Park, (414) 383-7066

Maritime Days
Veterans Park, (414) 223-7500
A celebration of Milwaukee's connection with the lake. Tour tall ships and U.S. Coast Guard boats. There's food, entertainment, and a midway.

River Flicks
Pere Marquette Park, Milwaukee, (414) 286-5700
Bring a blanket and watch a free movie under the stars.

Wisconsin State Fair
Wisconsin State Fair Park, West Allis, (414) 266-7000 or (800)884-FAIR

African World Festival
Henry Maier Festival Park, (414) 372-4567

River Jam
Milwaukee River banks, downtown Milwaukee,
(414) 286-5700
On Fridays the river banks come alive with music.

American Speed Association "Badgerland 150"
Milwaukee Mile, Tickets, (414) 453-8277
Short-track stock cars race on Milwaukee's track.

September

Al's Run and Walk
Milwaukee's Lakefront,
(414) 266-6320

Golden Guernsey's Heritage Farm Weekend
Milwaukee County Zoo, (414) 771-3040

Indian Summer Festival
Henry Maier Festival Park, (414) 774-7119
This is a chance to enjoy Native American dances,
crafts, and traditions.

Harvest Fair
Wisconsin State Fair Park, (414) 266-7000 or
(800)884-FAIR
This celebration of Wisconsin's farm background
has fresh produce, carnival rides, antique farm
machinery, food, and entertainment.

Renaissance Fair
Schlitz Audubon Center, (414) 352-2880
The medieval fun includes the King's Feast.

October

Fright Nights and The Halloween Spectacular
The Milwaukee County Zoo, (414) 771-3040

Wehr Nature Center's Halloween Haunt
Wehr Nature Center, (414) 425-8550
The center's trails become a forest of spooky fun.

November

Sinter Klausen
Trimborn Farm Park, (414) 273-8288
Celebrate Christmas with German traditions.

Milwaukee's Annual Christmas Parade
Wisconsin Avenue, (414) 272-1166

Holiday Folk Fair
The Wisconsin Center, Milwaukee, (414) 225-6225
Milwaukee's ethnic groups share their traditions.

December

Winterfest
Cathedral Square, Milwaukee, (414) 273-FEST
or (800)837-FEST

Firstar Eve
Milwaukee County, (414) 765-6500
Firstar Bank sponsors activities for kids, families,
and adults on New Year's Eve.

RESOURCE GUIDE: WHEN, WHAT, AND WHERE?

Although all of the sights listed in this guide offer programs for children and families, not all programs offered by these places are suitable. Before attending a theater production, it is a good idea to have your parents check to see if the program offered at that time is OK for you to see.

The information contained in this Resource Guide changes often. Call before you plan your trip for current days and hours of operation, as well as for admission prices.

If You Get Lost

Do you know what to do if you get lost? Make a plan with your parents about what to do if you lose them. If you forget what to do and you're in a store, go to a person working at a cash register. If you are outside, look for a mother with children. Tell her you are lost.

If there is an emergency and you need the police, fire department, or an ambulance, dial 911 from any phone. You won't need coins.

If you get separated from your family, pick up a phone and call 911.

Important Numbers

Injury, accident, fire, or emergency 911
Milwaukee Police Department (non-emergency)
(414) 933-4444
Greater Milwaukee Convention and Visitors
Bureau (414) 273-7222 or (800) 231-0903
Poison Center (800) 815-8855
Milwaukee County Sheriff (414) 278-4700

Transportation

Airport Transportation
Limousine Services (414) 769-9100
United Limo Inc. (414) 833-5555
Car Rental (national and airport numbers)
Avis (800) 831-2847 or (414) 744-2266
Budget (800) 527-0700 or (414) 541-8750
Econo-Car (414) 482-4570
Enterprise (800) 325-8007
Hertz (800) 654-3131 or (414) 747-5200
National (800) 227-7368 or (414) 483-9800
Milwaukee County Transit System
Schedule information (414) 344-6711
Sightseeing tour (414) 344-6711
Taxis
Airport Taxi Service (414) 791-3188
City Veterans Taxicab Cooperative
(414) 291-8080
General Mitchell Taxi Cab (414) 861-7555
Yellow Cab Co-op (414) 271-1800
Tour Boats
American Gondola (414) 272-7218
Celebration of Milwaukee (414) 278-1113
Edelweiss (414) 272-3625
Iroquois Harbor Cruises (414) 332-4194
Milwaukee River Boat Tours (414) 964-2628

Where They Are Located and When They're Open

African Hut Restaurant, 1107 North Old World Third Street, Milwaukee. Open Monday through Thursday 11:30 a.m. to 10 p.m., Friday and Saturday 11:30 a.m. to 11 p.m. Closed Sunday. (414) 765-1110

Annunciation Greek Orthodox Church, 9400 West Congress Street, Milwaukee. Designed by Frank Lloyd Wright. Public tours are given during the Greek Festival, the second weekend in July. (414) 461-9400

Applebee's Neighborhood Grill and Bar, 2500 North Mayfair Road, Wauwatosa, (414) 476-5771; 5900 North Port Washington Road, Glendale, (414) 963-0100; and 5100 South 76th Street, Greendale, (414) 423-8013. Open 11 a.m. daily.

Avalon Arts Coalition, Avalon Theater, 2473 South Kinnickinnic Avenue, Milwaukee. Performances given September through May. (414) 299-0752

Audubon Court Books Ltd., 383 West Brown Deer Road, Bayside. Open Sunday through Thursday 7 a.m. to 11 p.m., Friday and Saturday 7 a.m. to midnight. (414) 351-9140

Betty Brinn Children's Museum, 929 West Wisconsin Avenue, Milwaukee. Open Tuesday through Saturday from 9 a.m. to 5 p.m., Sunday from noon to 5 p.m. Closed Mondays. (414) 291-0888

Book Bay Children's Books, 415 East Silver Spring Drive, Whitefish Bay. Open Monday through Friday 10 a.m. to 5:30 p.m., Saturday 10 a.m. to 5 p.m. (414) 962-3444

Bradford Beach, 2400 North Lincoln Memorial Drive, Milwaukee.

Bradley Center, 1001 North Fourth Street, Milwaukee. Ticket information (414) 227-0400

Boerner Botanical Gardens, 5879 South 92nd Street, Whitnall Park, Hales Corners. Open daily 8 a.m. to sunset mid-April to October. Admission is free. (414) 425-1130

Brooks Stevens Automobile Collection, 10325 North Port Washington Road, Mequon. Open 9 a.m. to 5 p.m. weekdays, 10 a.m. to 3 p.m. Saturdays and Sundays. Closed Sundays from December 1 through March 1. (414) 425-1130

Buca Little Italy, 1233 North Van Buren Street, Milwaukee. Open Sunday through Thursday 5 p.m. to 10 p.m., Friday and Saturday 5 p.m. to 11 p.m. Reservations not accepted. (414) 224-8672

Cathedral Square, North Jackson and East Wells, Milwaukee.

Chuck E. Cheese, several locations: 2701 South Chase Avenue, Milwaukee, (414) 483-8655; 7401 West Good Hope Road, Milwaukee, (414) 358-2023; 2990 South 108 Street, West Allis, (414) 546-3600. Open Monday through Thursday 11 a.m. to 9 p.m., Friday 11 a.m. to 10 p.m., Saturday 10 a.m. to 10 p.m., Sunday 10 a.m. to 9 p.m.

Circus World Museum, 426 Water Street, Baraboo. From early May through mid-July, open daily between 9 a.m. and 6 p.m.; from mid-July through August, 9 a.m. and 9:30 p.m. From mid-September to early May, open Monday through Saturday between 9 a.m. and 5 p.m. and Sunday 11 a.m. and 5 p.m. (608) 356-8341. For recorded information call (608) 356-0800.

Cool Waters at Greenfield Park, 2028 South 124th Street, Milwaukee. Open Memorial Day through August 25 from noon to 8 p.m. Monday through Friday, and from noon to 6 p.m. on Saturdays, Sundays, and holidays. (414) 257-6100

Discovery World Museum, 712 West Wells Street, Milwaukee. Open daily 9 a.m. to 5 p.m. "Family Fusion" shows are free with admission to children between 6 and 12 accompanied by a parent. Children under 4 are not admitted to special shows because of the intensity of the performance. (414) 765-0777

DZ—Discovery Zone, 5008 South 74th Street, Greenfield. Open Sunday through Thursday 11 a.m. through 7 p.m., Friday and Saturday 10 a.m. to 9 p.m. Hours vary with seasons. Socks are required. (414) 281-3220

Ed Debevic's, 780 North Jefferson Street, Milwaukee. Open Sunday through Thursday 11 a.m. to 10 p.m., Friday and Saturday 11 a.m. to 11 p.m. (414) 226-2200

First Stage Milwaukee, Todd Wehr Theater, Marcus Center for the Performing Arts (formerly PAC). Season runs September through June. Call for performance schedules. (414) 273-7206 or (800) 472-4458

The Frederick C. Bogk House, 2420 Terrace Avenue, Milwaukee. Designed by Frank Lloyd Wright. A private residence. No tours.

Fun World, 198th and Bluemound Road, behind Tony Roma's Restaurant, Brookfield. Open Sunday through Thursday 11 a.m. to 10 p.m., Friday 11 a.m. to 11:30 p.m., and Saturday 10 a.m. to 11:30 p.m. Admission to activity areas varies. (414) 789-5370

General Mitchell International Airport, 5300 South Howell Avenue, Milwaukee. Send for the self-guided tour booklets or pick them up at the Administration Office. Guided tours for groups of 10 or more can be arranged by calling (414) 747-5300.

Gilles Frozen Custard Drive-In, 7515 West Blue Mound Road, (76th and Blue Mound) Wauwatosa. Open 10:30 a.m. to 11:30 p.m. from mid-June through August, 10:30 a.m. to 10:30 p.m. from September through mid-June. Closed from December 25 to mid-January. (414) 453-4875

The Grand Avenue Mall, 275 West Wisconsin Avenue, Milwaukee. (414) 224-0655

Green Meadows Farm, 23 miles southwest of Milwaukee on Highway 20 west of Waterford. From May 7 through June 28 tours are given from 10 a.m. to noon Tuesday through Friday and from 10 a.m. to 2 p.m. on Saturdays. From July 5 through September 1 tours are given from 10 a.m. to 2 p.m. Tuesdays through Sundays. From October 1 through October 28 tours are given from 9:30 a.m. to noon Monday through Friday and from 9:30 a.m. to 3 p.m. on Saturdays and Sundays. Afternoon tours for

groups of 20 or more by reservation only. (414) 534-2891

Hales Corners Speedway, 6531 South 108th Street, Franklin. Stock car racing. Open from the last Saturday in April through September. Qualifying is at 6:30 p.m. Races start at 7:30 p.m. (414) 425-4700

Henry Maier Festival Park, 200 N. Harbor Drive, Milwaukee.

High Rollers Skate Rental, Veteran's Park, North Lincoln Memorial Drive, Milwaukee. Open in good weather starting from late March to Memorial Day, weekends 10 a.m. to 8 p.m. Open seven days a week from Memorial Day to Labor Day. Open weekends from Labor Day to mid-October. (414) 273-1343

Humboldt Park Bandshell, 3000 South Howell Avenue, Milwaukee. Concerts free for everyone. (414) 257-6100

The International Clown Hall of Fame, Grand Avenue Mall. Open 10 a.m. to 4 p.m. daily. (414) 224-0655

Iroquois Harbor Cruises, dock in downtown Milwaukee, south of the Grand Avenue Mall on the west bank of the Milwaukee River between Michigan and Clybourn Street bridges. Cruises at 1 p.m. and 3 p.m. daily from mid-June through August. Call for reservations. (414) 332-4194

Johnson's Park, 7350 North 76th Street, Milwaukee. Open daily in good weather from early spring to mid-September from 10 a.m. to 10 p.m. Individual fees are charged for each activity like go-carts, mini golf, and batting cages. (414) 353-9548

Juneau Park Paddle Boats, Veteran's Park lagoon and Scout Lake. Open Saturdays, Sundays, and holidays in good weather from 10 a.m. to 8 p.m. (414) 217-7235

Kopp's Frozen Custard Stand, 7631 W. Layton Avenue, Greendale, and 5373 N. Port Washington Road, Glendale. Open from late June to early September from 10:30 a.m. to 11:30 p.m. Open from early September to late June, Monday through Friday 10:30 a.m. to 11 p.m. and Saturday until 11:30 p.m. (414) 282-4080

Lake Park, 3233 East Kenwood Boulevard, Milwaukee.

Leon's Frozen Custard Drive-In, 3131 South 27th Street, Milwaukee. Open Sunday through Thursday 11 a.m. to midnight, Friday until 12:30 p.m. and Saturday 1 a.m. (414) 383-1784

M & W Productions, P.O. Box 93910, Milwaukee. Plays presented at Cooley Auditorium, 1015 N. 6th Street. Plays presented in October, December, and May. (414) 272-7701

Mader's, 1037 North Old World Third Street, Milwaukee. Open Mondays 11:30 a.m. to 9 p.m.;

Tuesday, Wednesday and Thursday 11:30 a.m. to 10 p.m.; Friday and Saturday 11:30 a.m. to 11:30 p.m.; and Sunday 10:30 a.m. to 9 p.m. Reservations suggested. (800) 558-7171 or (414) 271-3377

Marcus Center for the Performing Arts (formerly the PAC), 929 North Water Street, Milwaukee. Box office: (414) 273-7206

Marquette Golden Eagles, NCAA basketball played at the Bradley Center. (414) 288-7127

Mayfair Mall, 2500 North Mayfair Road, Wauwatosa. (414) 711-1300

McKinley Beach and Marina, 1750 North Lincoln Memorial Drive, Milwaukee.

Mel's Diner, 3232 South 27th Street, Milwaukee. Open daily 6 a.m. to 12:30 a.m. (414) 389-9555

Milwaukee Art Museum, 750 North Lincoln Memorial Drive, Milwaukee. Open Tuesday, Wednesday, Friday and Saturday 10 a.m. to 5 p.m., Thursday noon to 9 p.m., Sunday noon to 5 p.m. Closed Mondays, January 1, Thanksgiving Day, and December 25. (414) 224-3220

Milwaukee Ballet Company, performances include classical and contemporary works. Ticket prices vary. (414) 643-7677

Milwaukee County Historical Center, 910 North Old World 3rd Street, Milwaukee. Open Monday through Friday 9:30 a.m. to 5 p.m., Saturday 10 a.m. to 5 p.m., Sunday 1 p.m. to 5 p.m. (414) 273-8288

Milwaukee County Park System, Special events line (414) 257-4503. Parks Information Line, (414) 257-6100.

Milwaukee County Stadium, 201 South 46th Street, Milwaukee.

Milwaukee County Zoo, 10001 West Blue Mound Road, Milwaukee. Open May 1 through September 9 a.m. to 5 p.m., October 1 through April 30 9 a.m. to 4:30 p.m. Parking is $5. (414) 771-3040

Milwaukee Maritime Center and Wisconsin Lake Schooner Education Association, 500 North Harbor Drive, Milwaukee. Open Monday through Saturday 8:30 a.m. to 5 p.m. Shipyard open Tuesday through Saturday. Donations accepted. (414) 276-7700

The Milwaukee Mile, State Fair Park, 7722 West Greenfield Avenue, West Allis. Box office, (414) 453-8277.

Milwaukee Public Museum, 800 West Wells Street, Milwaukee. Open daily 9 a.m. to 5 p.m. Closed Fourth of July, Thanksgiving Day, and Christmas Day. Recording of events, (414) 278-2702.

Milwaukee Symphony Orchestra, concerts presented September through June. (414) 291-6010

Milwaukee Wave, games played at the Bradley Center. (414) 243-4625

Miss Katie's Diner, 1900 West Clybourn, Milwaukee. Open Monday through Friday 7 a.m. to 10:30 p.m., Saturday 8 a.m. to 11 p.m. and Sunday 9 a.m. to 8 p.m. (414) 344-0044

Mitchell Park Horticultural Conservatory (The Domes), 524 South Layton Boulevard, Milwaukee. Open daily 9 a.m. to 5 p.m. including Sundays and holidays. (414) 649-9800

Old World Wisconsin, S103 W37890 Highway 67, Eagle. Open weekdays 10 a.m. to 4 p.m. and weekends during May, June, September, and October 10 a.m. to 5 p.m. During July and August open daily 10 a.m. to 5 p.m. (414) 594-6300

Olsen Planetarium, 1900 E. Kenwood Boulevard, Milwaukee. Programs are offered at 7 p.m. and 8:15 p.m. on Fridays during the University's school year. Children must be 6 years or older to attend. (414) 229-4961

Pabst Theater, 144 East Wells Street, Milwaukee. Ticket prices vary per performance. (414) 278-3663

Pabst Mansion, 2000 West Wisconsin Avenue, Milwaukee. Open daily 10 a.m. to 3:30 p.m., Sunday noon to 3:30 p.m. Closed on holidays. (414) 931-0808

Pettit National Ice Center, Gate 6 on 84th Street, Wisconsin State Fair Park, I-94 and 84th Street, West Allis. Hours vary. (414) 266-0100

Renaissance Book Shop, 834 North Plankinton Avenue, Milwaukee. Open Monday through Friday noon to 7 p.m., Saturday noon to 5 p.m. (414) 271-6850

River Falls, 5401 West Layton Avenue, Greenfield. Open daily from mid-April through mid-October in good weather 10 a.m. to 11 p.m. Activity fees vary. (414) 281-2815

Rollaero Skate Center, 5200 South Pennsylvania Avenue, Cudahy. Call for information on sessions. Roller skate rental available. (414) 747-1414

St. Joan of Arc Chapel, Marquette University Campus, 14th Street and Wisconsin Avenue, Milwaukee. Open daily 10 a.m. to 4 p.m. (414) 288-6873

Saint Josaphat Basilica, 2336 South 6th Street, Milwaukee. Tours by appointment. (414) 645-5623

Schlitz Audubon Center, 1111 East Brown Deer Road, Bayside. Open Tuesdays through Sundays 9 a.m. to 5 p.m. (414) 352-2880. "Nature Now" 24-hour recorded information line, 352-8833.

Scout Heritage Museum/Boy Scout Council Office, 330 South 84th Street, Milwaukee. Open daily noon to 4 p.m. (414) 774-1776

Harry W. Schwartz Booksellers, four locations: 209 East Wisconsin Avenue, Milwaukee, (414) 274-6400; 4093 North Oakland Avenue, Shorewood, (414) 963-3111. 17145 West Bluemound Road, Brookfield, (414) 797-6140; and 10976 North Port Washington Road, Mequon, (414) 241-6220.

Skate University, 10928 West Oklahoma Avenue, West Allis. Call for open skate hours and special event information. (414) 545-8444

Solid Gold McDonalds, 5040 South 76th Street, Greenfield. (414) 282-6480

Timber Wolf Preservation Society, 6669 South 76th Street, Greendale. Open Saturday and Sunday 10 a.m. to 3 p.m. (414) 425-6107

Trimborn Farm Park, South 84th and West Grange Avenues, Greendale. The farm is open Tuesdays and Thursdays 9 a.m. to 1 p.m. No admission fee. The picnic grounds are always open. Call for information on special activities. (414) 332-7275

Washington Park Bandshell, 1859 North 40th Street, Milwaukee. (414) 257-6100

Wehr Nature Center, 9701 West College Avenue, Franklin. Part of Whitnall Park. Open daily 8 a.m. to 4:30 p.m. (414) 425-8550

West Allis Farmers' Market, between 65th and 66th Street on National Avenue. Open Tuesdays,

Thursdays, and Saturdays from 1 p.m. to 4 p.m. May through November. During winter open 10 a.m. to 1 p.m.

Whitnall Park, 5879 South 92nd Street, Hales Corners. Open Daily.

Wilson Park Recreation Center, 1601 West Howard Avenue, Milwaukee. Grounds open daily. The hours for public ice-skating vary. Call for times. Recording of public skating times, (414) 281-6289. To find out when the Milwaukee Admirals are practicing, call (414) 281-6289.

Willows, 4241 South 27th Street, Milwaukee. Open April 1 through September 15, 10 a.m. to 10 p.m., weather permitting. (414) 282-1221

Wisconsin Center (formerly MECCA), 500 West Kilbourn Avenue, Milwaukee. Recording of current events, (414) 271-2750.

Wisconsin Maritime Museum and Wisconsin Lake Schooner Education Association, 500 North Harbor Drive, Milwaukee. Open Monday through Saturday 8:30 a.m. to 5 p.m. Shipyard is open Tuesday through Saturday. (414) 276-7700

Wisconsin State Fair Park, 8100 West Greenfield Avenue, West Allis. (414) 266-7188 or (800) 884-FAIR

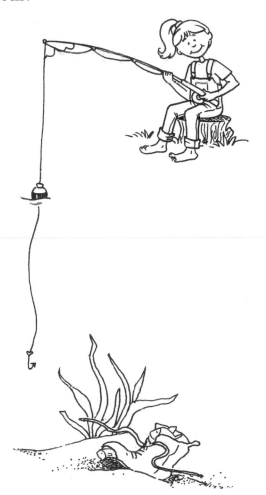

ANSWERS TO PUZZLES

ACROSS	DOWN
3. TRACK	1. COAL
6. LAWRENCE	2. STEEL
7. FISH	4. MICHIGAN
8. PORT	5. GREAT
9. GRAIN	

page 15

page 17

page
19

page
21

page
23

```
A P S S A R A I N F O R E S T
B A I W O Q W S A E D B A N T
A L V L K F W J S S E V D N V
X M P A M C A C T U S X S O I
B T L C D A J L E O E O R O O
V R E E A R L S G A R E F K L
B E S L J A S Z U Y T B L I E
N E Y C N H T E L A J L Z K T
J D A A H E I R W I K O T E S
V H N K E Y T F O F L O W E R
G A L A O V E O B E L M E W W
B O S H T S G R O W Z O S T W
```

page
25

page
31

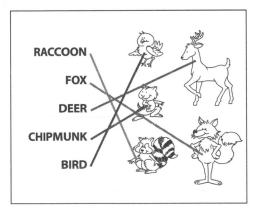

page
33

RACCOON

FOX

DEER

CHIPMUNK

BIRD

ACROSS

2. LEAF
4. TREES
5. MICE
6. TRACKS
7. HORNED
8. ACORNS

DOWN

1. NESTS
3. DEER
5. MUSHROOM

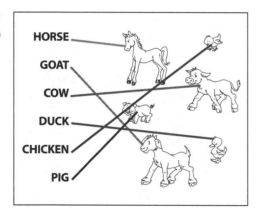

HORSE
GOAT
COW
DUCK
CHICKEN
PIG

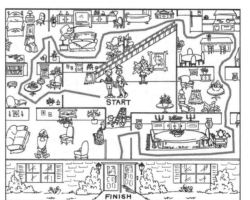

START

FINISH

page
63

ACROSS

3. BANGO
4. HOOP
6. NET
7. STREET

DOWN

1. COURT
2. COACH
3. BRADLEY
5. POINTS
8. TEAM

page
69

page
65

page
75

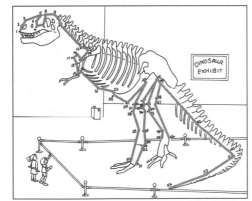

page
77

page
81

X	T	Y	F	K	H	K	O	Q	F	X	F	J	W	Q	G	J
W	K	X	M	K	G	W	F	X	A	G	S	K	W	Y	F	G
K	A	Y	K	L	X	K	J	J	F	Y	X	V	Q	Y	X	W
W	A	J	F	K	X	F	E	J	K	Y	G	Y	G	X	Y	X
J	Y	W	D	X	I	G	X	Y	G	F	S	K	F	G	W	
G	X	Y	X	X	O	F	W	F	K	G	X	Y	N	Y	G	K

Hidden message:

Thomas Alva Edison

page
83

A	M	N	E	C	K	E	R	C	H	I	E	F	H	A
T	C	O	N	F	R	E	A	B	L	S	A	S	B	P
O	A	B	O	F	G	C	R	B	U	B	K	O	P	O
T	K	D	A	L	J	A	S	T	N	A	M	O	S	S
E	F	X	K	D	T	N	K	T	I	A	P	E	Z	T
M	G	A	F	S	G	O	E	L	F	H	A	T	S	C
P	V	Z	O	B	S	E	T	C	O	Z	F	M	A	A
O	W	J	A	A	K	B	S	T	R	E	U	X	J	R
L	B	U	C	K	S	K	I	N	M	R	U	Y	H	D
E	A	Q	U	M	I	S	T	L	D	A	I	Z	O	S
O	L	A	A	D	L	B	C	E	R	E	P	G	B	A
E	T	X	C	W	H	E	A	D	D	R	E	S	S	L

page
85

page
91

page
93

page 97

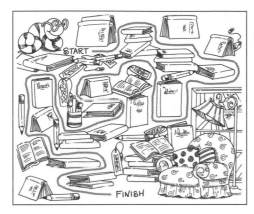

page 99

```
Z R H E G R L E C D E N R F O
B L U E B E R R I E S V A H G
E O H F E R T I D I T E S M O
P A P P L E S E E B O S P B L
D T O O R E S S R B M N B G B
S B T T H M T E B K A A E X A
S Y A R S D B T G N T V R T U
D T T A E W E I U U O L R E L
Q L O I C C A Q U C H P I W N
O M Y J U K N L V A E R E H S
C A R R O T S E S Q U A S H C
R Z T T R B E T P U L I M E K
```

page 101

page 107

page 109

```
C R H E V G O U D A E R L F O
W H N A V M N E S O P Q Y P G
A O E F E I T I L J Z E R R O
M W N D S L H E R B A S S O L
E T P S D D S S D B T C T V B
R B T T O A J E B W E A K O A
R I Y T S H A R P V N E I G L U
I C T S A E W D I H U I L Y O L
A L F M U E N S T E R P O N N
N M Y J U K R L V A P R A E S
U I S E I S T E S W I S S O C
R C O L B Y U L I Z E K
```

page 111

GEOGRAPHICAL INDEX: WHERE IS EVERYTHING?

Milwaukee's Lakefront
Betty Brinn Children's Museum
Bradford Beach
Celebration of Milwaukee
Henry Maier Festival Park
McKinley Marina
McKinley Beach
Milwaukee Maritime Center and
    Wisconsin Lake Schooner
    Education Association
O'Donnell Park
Port of Milwaukee
Veterans Park
War Memorial and Milwaukee Art
    Museum

Downtown
The African Hut
American Gondola
Bradley Center
Buca Little Italy
Cathedral Square
Discovery World Museum
Ed Debevic's
The Grand Avenue Mall
IMAX Theater
Mader's Restaurant
Marcus Center for the
    Performing Arts
Marquette University
Milwaukee County Historical Center
Milwaukee Public Museum
Miss Katie's Diner
Old World Third Street
Pabst Mansion
Pabst Theater
Pere Marquette Park
Riverwalk

St. Joan of Arc Chapel
Wisconsin Center

North of Downtown Milwaukee
Applebee's
Audubon Court Books
Book Bay Children's Books
Brooks Stevens Automobile
    Collection
Havenwoods State Forest
Kopp's Frozen Custard Stand
Lake Park
North Point Water Tower
Schlitz Audubon Center
University of Wisconsin - Milwaukee

South of Downtown Milwaukee
Allen Bradley Clock Tower
Avalon Theater
Chuck E. Cheese
General Mitchell International
    Airport
Humboldt Park Bandshell
Mitchell Park Horticultural
    Conservatory, "The Domes"
Mitchell Park
Rollaero
Wilson Park

West of Downtown Milwaukee
Applebee's
Fun World

Gilles Frozen Custard Drive-In
Heritage Museum
Mayfair Mall
Milwaukee County Zoo
Milwaukee County Stadium
The Milwaukee Mile
Skate University
Washington Park Bandshell
West Allis Farmers Market
Wisconsin State Fair Park

Northwest Milwaukee County
Johnson's Park Chuck E. Cheese
Northridge Shopping Center

Southwest of Downtown Milwaukee
Applebee's
Boerner Botanical Garden
Chuck E. Cheese
Cool Waters at Greenfield Park
DZ
Hales Corners Speedway
Kopp's Frozen Custard
Leon's Frozen Custard Drive-In
Mel's Diner
River Falls
Scout Lake
Solid Gold McDonalds
Southridge Shopping Mall
Timber Wolf Preservation Society
Willows
Wehr Nature Center
Whitnall Park

INDEX

A

African American Children's Theater, 100
African Hut, 104, 106
Allen Bradley Clock Tower, 44
Annunciation Greek Orthodox Church, 50
Applebee's, 108
Audubon Court Books, 96
Avalon Arts Coalition, 100
Avalon Theater, 100

B

Betty Brinn Children's Museum, 78
Boerner Botanical Gardens, 26
Book Bay Children's Books, 96
Bookstores, 96
Bradford Beach, 18
Bradley Center, 58, 62
Brooks Stevens Automobile Collection, 72
Buca Little Italy, 106

C

Children's Theater, 100
Chuck E. Cheese, 108
City Ballet Theater, 102
City Hall, 42
Concerts in the Park, 12, 102
Cool Waters, 94
County Stadium, 60
Curiocity, 88
Custard stands, 112

D

Din-o-mite, 64
dinosaurs, 74
Discovery World, 80
Discovery Zone, 70

E

East Side, 50
Ed Debevic's, 110
ENERGEE, 62
Ethnic Crossroads Village, 86

F

Festival City Symphony, 102
First Stage Milwaukee, 100
Firstar Center, 42
Frederick C. Bogk House , 50
Fun World, 70

G

General Mitchell International Airport, 54
German Fest, 2
Gift of Wings, 14
Gilles, 112
Golden Eagles, 62
Grand Avenue Mall, 90
Great Circus Parade, 2
Green Meadows Farm, 38
Greenfield Park, 94

H

Hales Corners Speedway, 58
Harry W. Schwartz Bookshops, 96
Havenwoods State Forest, 34
Henry Maier Festival Park, 52, 88
High Rollers, 14
Hoan Bridge, 6, 52
Hyatt-Regency Hotel, 42

I

International Clown Hall of Fame, 76
Iroquois Harbor Cruises, 92

J

Johnson's Park, 70

K

Ko Thi Dance Company, 102
Kopp's, 112

L

Lakefront Festival, 46
Lake Michigan, 1, 10, 16, 28, 92
Lake Park, 10, 20
Leon's Frozen Custard, 112
Light Waves and Laser Beams, 80

M

M&W Productions, 100
Mader's, 106
Marquette University, 24, 56
McKinley Beach, 1, 16
McKinley Marina, 16
Mel's Diner, 110
Miller Park, 60
Milwaukee Art Museum, 46
Milwaukee Ballet, 102
Milwaukee Brewers, 60
Milwaukee Bucks, 62
Milwaukee Community Sailing Center, 14
Milwaukee County Historical Center, 72
Milwaukee County Park System, 12
Milwaukee County Zoo, 30
Milwaukee Maritime Center, 84
Milwaukee Mile, 58, 66
Milwaukee Public Museum, 74
Milwaukee Public Theater, 100
Milwaukee Symphony Orchestra, 102
Milwaukee Wave, 64
Milwaukee Youth Theater, 100

Miss Katie's Diner, 110
Mitchell Gallery of Flight, 54
Mitchell Park Horticultural
    Conservatory, 22
Mitchell Park and "The Domes," 22

N
North Point Lighthouse, 20
North Point Water Tower, 50

O
Oak Leaf Trail, 12, 14
Old World Wisconsin, 86
Olsen Planetarium, 72
Oriental Theater, 50

P
Pabst Mansion, 48
Pajama Jamborees, 102
Peace Mural, 54
Pere Marquette Park, 24
Pettit National Ice Training Center, 68,
    70
Plankinton Building, 90
Polar Bear Club, 18
Polaris Puppet Theater, 100

Port of Milwaukee, 6, 52
Pro Beach Volleyball Tournament, 18

R
R&D Cafe, 80
Rainbow Summer, 102
Red Nose Productions, 100
Renaissance Book Shop, 96
Rieder, Jim, 40
Ringling Bros. Circus, 76
River Falls, 70
RiverSplash, 102
Riverwalk, 24
Rollaero, 70

S
Schlitz Audubon Center, 28, 32
Scout Heritage Museum, 82
Scout Lake, 36
Skate University, 70
Solid Gold McDonald's, 108
St. Joan of Arc Chapel, 56
St. Josaphat's Basilica, 4
St. Lawrence Seaway, 6
Streetlife, 62
Summerfest, 2, 3, 64

T
Timber Wolf Preservation Society, 40
Trimborn Farm Park, 72

U
University of Wisconsin-Milwaukee, 50,
    72

V
Veteran's Park, 14

W
War Memorial Center, 46
Weather, 10
Wehr Nature Center, 26
West Allis Farmers' Market, 98
Whitnall Park, 26
Willows, 70
Wilson Park, 70
Winterfest, 2
Wisconsin Center, 88
Wisconsin Gas Building, 42
Wisconsin Lake Schooner Education
    Association, 84
Wisconsin State Fair Park, 88

PHOTO CREDITS

Pages i, 102—Linda Kimpel; Pages 6, 12, 20, 22, 46, 52, 56, 58, 74, 78, 80, 86—Greater Milwaukee Convention & Visitors Bureau; Pages iii (left), 28, 32(top)—David Stokes/Schlitz Audubon Center; Page iii (right), 14, 36, 70—Milwaukee County Parks; Pages 1, 3, 4, 10, 16, 24, 42, 90, 104—David Lahaye/Department of City Development; Page 2—Jim Morrill; Page 6—Port of Milwaukee; Page 8—Harley-Davidson; Pages 18, 50 (bottom), 98—Milwaukee Journal Sentinel; Page 26—R. Schmidt; Page 30—M.A. Nedder/Milwaukee County Zoo; Page 32 (bottom)—Dr. J.W. Franta/Schlitz Audubon Center; Page 34—Havenwoods Staff; Page 40—Timber Wolf Preservation Society; Page 44—Rockwell Automation; Page 48—Captain Frederick Pabst Mansion; Page 54—Mitchell Airport; Page 60—Major League Baseball Properties/Joe Picciolo; Page 62—Noren Trotman/NBA Photos Inc.; Page 64 (bottom)—Suzanne Rubey; Page 64 (top)—Everett Kamikawa; Page 66—Dan Boyd; Page 68—Pettit National Ice Center; Page 72—Milwaukee County Historical Society; Page 76—International Clown Hall of Fame; Page 82—Boy Scouts of America; Pages ii, 84—Wisconsin Lake Schooner Education Association; Page 88—Rutley; Page 92—Iroquois Harbor Cruises; Page 94—Cool Waters at Greenfield Park; Page 96—Harry Schwartz Booksellers; Page 100—First Stage Milwaukee; Page 106—Pete Arvan; Page 108—Solid Gold McDonald's; Page 110—Janice Ulrich/Miss Katie's Diner; Page 112—Leon Corporation.

American Origins Series

Each is 48 pages and $12.95 hardcover.
Tracing Our English Roots
Tracing Our German Roots
Tracing Our Irish Roots
Tracing Our Italian Roots
Tracing Our Japanese Roots
Tracing Our Jewish Roots
Tracing Our Polish Roots

Bizarre & Beautiful Series

Each is 48 pages, $14.95 hardcover, $9.95 paperback.
Bizarre & Beautiful Ears
Bizarre & Beautiful Eyes
Bizarre & Beautiful Feelers
Bizarre & Beautiful Noses
Bizarre & Beautiful Tongues

Extremely Weird® Series

Each is 32 pages and $5.95 paperback.
Extremely Weird Animal Defenses
Extremely Weird Animal Disguises
Extremely Weird Animal Hunters
Extremely Weird Bats
Extremely Weird Endangered Species
Extremely Weird Fishes
Extremely Weird Frogs
Extremely Weird Reptiles
Extremely Weird Spiders
Extremely Weird Birds
Extremely Weird Insects
Extremely Weird Mammals
Extremely Weird Micro Monsters
Extremely Weird Primates
Extremely Weird Sea Creatures
Extremely Weird Snakes

Kidding Around®
Travel Series

Each is 144 pages and $7.95 paperback.
Kidding Around Atlanta
Kidding Around Austin
Kidding Around Boston
Kidding Around Cleveland
Kids Go! Denver
Kidding Around Indianapolis
Kidding Around Kansas City
Kidding Around Miami
Kidding Around Milwaukee
Kidding Around Minneapolis/St. Paul
Kidding Around San Francisco
Kids Go! Seattle
Kidding Around Washington, D.C.

Kids Explore Series

Written by kids for kids, each is $9.95 paperback.
Kids Explore America's African American Heritage, 160 pages
Kids Explore America's Hispanic Heritage, 160 pages
Kids Explore America's Japanese American Heritage, 160 pages
Kids Explore America's Jewish Heritage, 160 pages
Kids Explore Kids Who Make a Difference, 128 pages
Kids Explore the Gifts of Children with Special Needs, 128 pages
Kids Explore the Heritage of Western Native Americans, 128 pages

Rough and Ready Series

Each is 48 pages and $4.95 paperback.
Rough and Ready Homesteaders
Rough and Ready Cowboys
Rough and Ready Loggers
Rough and Ready Outlaws and Lawmen
Rough and Ready Prospectors
Rough and Ready Railroaders

X-ray Vision Series

Each is 48 pages and $6.95 paperback.
Looking Inside the Brain
Looking Inside Cartoon Animation
Looking Inside Caves and Caverns
Looking Inside Sports Aerodynamics
Looking Inside Sunken Treasure
Looking Inside Telescopes and the Night Sky

Ordering Information

Please check your local bookstore for our books, or call **1-800-888-7504** to order direct and to receive a complete catalog. A shipping charge will be added to your order total.

Send all inquiries to:
John Muir Publications
P.O. Box 613, Santa Fe, NM 87504

M&W Productions Children's Theatre

P.O. Box 93910
Milwaukee, WI 53203
414-272-7701

HALF OFF!

Expires 9/15/99

Buy one full-price 97/98 or 98/99 season ticket and receive 1/2 off second ticket. Redeem by mail with payment and SASE. Call for performance location. Not valid with other discounts.

KIDDING AROUND® MILWAUKEE

First Stage Milwaukee

Marcus Center for the Performing Arts
929 N. Water Street
Milwaukee, WI 53202
414-273-7206

TWO FOR THE PRICE OF ONE!

Expires 9/15/99

Receive one free child's admission with paid adult admission to any Saturday performance. Holiday production excluded. Redeem in person/by mail at Marcus Center box office.

KIDDING AROUND® MILWAUKEE

Milwaukee Symphony Orchestra

Marcus Center for the Performing Arts
929 N. Water Street
Milwaukee, WI 53202
414-273-7206

TWO FOR THE PRICE OF ONE!

Expires 9/15/99

Buy one Kinderkonzert single ticket and receive one child's ticket free. Valid for 97/98 or 98/99 season. Redeem in person at Marcus box office. (Subject to availability. Not valid on previously purchased tickets. Not redeemable for cash.)

KIDDING AROUND® MILWAUKEE

Avalon Arts Coalition

Avalon Theatre
2473 S. Kinnickinnic Ave.
Milwaukee, WI 53207
414-744-2451

$1.75 VALUE!

Expires 9/15/99

Buy one admission and receive one free.

KIDDING AROUND® MILWAUKEE

Chuck E. Cheese's

Milwaukee: 414-483-8655
West Allis: 414-546-3600
Brookfield: 414-782-5530

$10 VALUE!

Expires 9/15/99

One large 2 topping pizza or Super Combo, 4 cups of soft drinks & 30 game & ride tokens just $17.99 with coupon.

KIDDING AROUND® MILWAUKEE

Ed Debevic's

780 N. Jefferson St.
Milwaukee, WI
414-226-2200

TWO FOR THE PRICE OF ONE!

Expires 9/15/99

Buy one hot fudge sundae and receive a second one free.

KIDDING AROUND® MILWAUKEE